Stage Lights

Lighting up your purpose and unleashing your inner Rock Star

JONELLE MARIE CARTER

*Stage Lights: Lighting up your purpose and
unleashing your inner Rock Star*
Copyright © 2024 by Jonelle Marie Carter
All rights reserved.
First Edition: 2024

Cover Photo: Amanda Wilson
Cover design and Formatting: Streetlight Graphics

No part of this book may be reproduced, scanned, or distributed in any printed or electronic form without permission. Please do not participate in or encourage piracy of copyrighted materials in violation of the author's rights. Thank you for respecting the hard work of this author.

"To the women who have fueled my fire: my mom, Jo Ellen, who taught me to never back down from my dreams; and my daughter, Marleyna, who gives me a reason to keep running towards them."

Thank You

Table of Contents

Chapter 1:
Hey, Don't I Know You? (Remembering who you were as a kid) Guiding you to remember and uncover yourself and your dreams 1

Chapter 2:
Hey Little Caterpillar (Shedding your outer layer) Guiding you to shed the protective cover that shields the real you 10

Chapter 3:
Well That's Pretty Gutsy (Leaving a life that is no longer serving you and never looking back) Guiding you to plan for big change 21

Chapter 4:
Don't Tell Me What To Do- But Tell Me It's Ok (Learning to stop needing approval from others and staying confident when things start to happen) Guiding you how to stay confident when the big change starts to occur 32

Chapter 5:
Rock N' Roll (When you are on a roll) Guiding you to create anything that you can dream of 42

Chapter 6:
Can I Get A Selfie With You? (And other ways that people will want to learn all of your ways) Guiding you how to teach other to continue the flow of awesomeness 64

Conclusion 83

"May you find the strength to leap fearlessly, unlocking the doors to the extraordinary life that awaits when you live in alignment with your most authentic self."

Dear Reader,

Prepare to unleash the most unapologetically fabulous version of yourself! Welcome to the extraordinary journey of discovering your gifts and using them to live your healthiest, happiest life—because, love, you deserve nothing less.

Buckle up—this ain't your typical self-help book. We're about to dive headfirst into a sea of sparkle and sass, leaving behind doubts and insecurities in our wake. Together, we'll uncover the untapped potential that lies within you, waiting to shine like a dazzling diamond.

Gone are the days of conforming to expectations and settling for mediocre. It's time to own your brilliance and embrace everything that makes you unique. This book isn't here to tell you how to change yourself—no way, honey! We're here to unearth your true essence, to empower you to amplify your natural talents and gifts.

From uncovering your hidden passions to embracing your flaws as a badge of honor, we will navigate the winding path of self-discovery with relentless sass. Expect laughter, empowerment, and a splash of glitter, because let's face it—life is too short for anything less fabulous.

In these pages, you'll find practical tips, juicy anecdotes, and fierce exercises that will push you out of your comfort zone and into a whole new territory of self-love and self-worth. Get ready to say goodbye to self-doubt and hello to a life bursting with light and satisfaction.

So, darling, if you're ready to ditch the mundane and spark your inner firework, step into these pages and let's embark on the most extraordinary journey of your life.

Together, we'll redefine what it means to live your healthiest, happiest life—the sassy way.

Buckle up, baby, because we're about to set your world on fire!

Let's GLOW!

xo Jmc

Dear Mom and Dad,

All my life I've had brown carpet. Here are the reasons that I would like new carpet.

1. Brown carpet is ugly.

Love, your daughter,
Jonelle (six years old)

P.S. I hate my name.

This is one of the many examples of my first writings that popped up as a memory on the heels of our daughter presenting us with a slideshow. While my letter was about brown carpet, my daughter's presentation was about why we should let her have a pet turtle. When I shared the slideshow with my parents, the text I received back was a simple: "Oh boy, Jonelle #2."

I have been pleading my case since I was old enough to talk. I also had an issue with my name since about the same time, which is ironic because I married a man whose ex wife has the same first *and* middle name as me…or maybe I have the same name as her. I guess we will leave well enough alone and just be happy that God gave Terry two wives with the same name, since his memory isn't always the greatest, and somehow the heavens protected him from ever screwing it up in bed.

I was a powerhouse of a kid. Full of sugar and spice and

everything nice…but heavy on the spice. I was a presenter, petitioner, idea savvy, no-means-yes-and-yes-means-no kind of a girl. I had *big* ideas before I was even old enough to realize how big they were. I planned on huge success and would close my eyes at night, dreaming about how excited I was to get there. I was fueled by passion and feasted on everything my mind would allow me to be. No doubts, just pure excitement to grow up and become everything I could dream of and, of course, pick out pink carpet and *never* allow a square inch of ugly brown carpet to be laid in any corner of my castle.

Of course, as I got older those ideas were slowly buried inside of me in fear of being the weird kid. You've been there, right? "Hey guys, what if we _____ and pretend we are _____."

You're wide-eyed, chomping at the bit to see how excited your friends are going to be that you've come up with this super creative and fun idea…only to be met with crickets and side-eyes that seemed to say, "Um…that idea is dorky," or worse yet, "that's for babies."

Ugh. The worst. This is why I ended up being the dog when my girlfriends and I played house on the playground and recess. This is why I dropped out of band after graduating the eighth grade. This is also why people were shocked when I became a singer and even more shocked when I wrote my first book. I spent a good chunk of my life hiding who I was. What my passions were and what my purpose was. This led me down a long and winding road of bad relationships, bad jobs, really bad insecurities, and some pretty terrible decisions. Lost, wandering, searching for the little me who the twenty-something me buried deep in sticky lip gloss and uncomfortable high heels. Desperately calling out for the girl who carried the spice around and sprinkled it liberally over everything she touched. I had gone from hot pepper to sodium-free salt substitute.

The problem with growing up is that we become aware of our differences, which then make us feel…well, different. When we feel different, we try to fit in, and by doing so, we erase everything that makes us, us.

I remember my first homecoming dance my freshman year. A group of six of us went to the local truck stop after the dance, and it was the first time I had been in a setting with high school kids who were older than me. They all ordered the same sandwich: the "Hickory Dickory Dock," which was a grilled chicken breast sandwich covered in barbecue sauce, bacon, and American cheese. Gross. I hated American cheese, not a huge fan of barbecue sauce, and didn't really love chicken sandwiches to be truthful. But I was too afraid to order something different. So I just said, "I'll have the same," and choked down a sandwich that I still shudder thinking about to this day. The only part of that sandwich I liked was the bacon, and even that was undercooked. (Where are my crispy bacon siblings at? Yeah baby. If you know, you know.)

This started the first of many many "yes" situations that should have been a big fat "no." Just to fit in, which denied my identity. Anything not to be judged. Anything not to be different.

When we do this enough to our impressionable minds, we become someone who we don't recognize anymore, and so begins our search to "find ourselves." By the time we hit our—oh, let's say mid twenties, something starts pulling inside just a bit. By the time we are coming around to that thirtieth margarita-filled birthday, the pull is really starting to show up, and by the time we land at forty, we are worn out because we have spent the last two decades ignoring and pushing it way down deep and letting it fester, which in turn causes things like depression, anxiety, illness, weight gain, and a constant rattle in our souls that is finally too loud to ignore anymore.

It is my belief that we are all born into this world with a purpose. A gift. A talent. It is that belief that my coaching business and the heart behind everything that I do has been built upon. It is also that belief that has changed my entire adult life, allowing me to live in alignment with my true purpose, fall in love with my work, and look forward to every single day.

I once read a quote that said "Life is too short to be working toward someone else's dream." Read that again. Who you were meant to be is in there. She never left. She was just buried under someone else's dream, and now it's time to pay attention to the pull. It's time to bring that little girl with the big dreams and that hate of brown carpet back up to the surface and put her in charge. It's time to uncover and rediscover your *why*, and when you do, you will start to see *big* changes fast. When you give yourself back to yourself you become whole again and everything lines back up. Clear heart, clear mind, clear vision.

You are probably reading this and trying to figure out exactly how you're supposed to make a big life change when you are already incredibly stressed with your life. Well, here's the thing. You are either going to have stress where you are and you'll be exactly in the same place day after day, or you are going to have stress by moving forward while you open up doors and opportunities day after day. Choose your stress.

Think of this book as your personal coach. Your bestie. Your guide to becoming exactly who you are meant to be. I will be your compadre, your compass, and your worst nightmare at times. (I won't let you give up even when you want to, and that might piss you off…but too bad. You're not quitting now!) This isn't going to be easy work, growing and getting to know your true self, but once you start to blossom, there will be no stopping you. You will finally have the ability to see your gifts with crystal-clear clarity and you will be a happier, healthier version of the person who once couldn't even see past her own front door.

Welcome to the journey back to YOU. You are going to love it here.

Chapter 1:

HEY, DON'T I KNOW YOU? (REMEMBERING WHO YOU WERE AS A KID) GUIDING YOU TO REMEMBER AND UNCOVER YOURSELF AND YOUR DREAMS

Close your eyes with me and imagine this scene playing out.

It's the summer of 1989. The hot sun is beating down on your parents' brown Oldsmobile Cutlass Supreme, which is parked sideways in your front yard, drying off after you, your dad, and your little brother handwashed it with Dawn dish soap and a yellow sponge in the shape of a figure eight. In the distance, you hear the scraping of metal roller skate wheels on the pavement, indicating the neighbor two doors down, who is pretty much your other sibling, is finished with chores and ready to hang out. You grab your Schwinn with the banana seat and white wicker basket and peddle fast down the broken sidewalk, whose bumps you can still anticipate thirty-something years later. The warm wind is blowing in your hair. The in-between neighbor has a package of Oscar Mayer hot dogs on a charcoal grill and is stirring up an orange tupperware pitcher of grape Kool-Aid with the full two cups of real white sugar. None of that Crystal Lite action. Stevia who?

You and your two-doors-down neighbor meet up. Bike thrown into the olive-green grass, blades pop up between bare little toes. Gates swing open and the backyard acts as a blank canvas for imaginations to turn it into something grand are open and ready for its next adventure.

As the sun continues its daily journey to the west, a stage is being set in the backyard. Bedsheets are being pulled off of the clothesline and thrown back over tent-style to make a backdrop, rocks dug up to be used as weights to keep the corners down. Scripts are being written, parts handed out. Stagehand instructions are being announced to the younger siblings and bossy neighbor (that's me), who knows exactly what she is envisioning and wants out of this backyard production; she's stomping her feet because two-doors-down neighbor has lost interest, and now she has lost her supporting-role actor.

I think it's clear to see that I was a creator from the start. When I look back on those days, it never ceases to amaze me how crystal clear my love of making something out of nothing was. It also never ceases to amaze me how far I would bury that love and have to fight to find it again later in life. How did something that was so much a part of me become so foreign in my teens and twenties?

Let me ask you this: if someone told you that you could be head over heels in love with your job, make a great living, and live a beautiful abundant life doing what you loved to do as a kid, would you believe them? Would you have believed them in fourth grade? Or how about your freshman year in college? Would you have felt supported in all of your dreams and crazy ideas? Or would you have felt like you needed to pick something that maybe let you fit in a little more. Or maybe *seemed* a little more secure. Or grown-up. Or maybe something that followed more closely in the footsteps of your family? Were all of your friends picking out majors that were alphabetized in the tiny cinder block room that housed your high school guidance counselor's office? Was your GUIDANCE counselor even living a life that they were head over heels in love with?

As we get older we become used to the grind. Part of the system. We go to school. We are taught what the state *says* we need to be taught. We are graded and ranked by how well we fit into that criteria. Then the criteria makes new criteria for what and who we are supposed to become. No more makeshift stages, at least not for your "real" job… and little by little who you were when you were young and dreamy disappears into who you are expected to become.

Now don't get me wrong. If "guidance counselor" is on your dream job list, then please go for it and put your all into hitting that goal, because we need all of the people. All of the gifts. All of the talents, and we absolutely need amazing guidance counselors who will see the potential in each and every student and show them where their opportunity is. If it's fire twirling that tickles your fancy, then girl, twirl away!

Uncovering and digging up your carefree self and all of those big dreams is going to take some work. You're going to have to get uncomfortable and relive a few things in order to learn how to live for real…but why is it so important to remember your kid self?

Well for one, living a life that isn't authentic to who

you are is exhausting. It will break you down and leave you looking for fulfillment in other ways. Food, relationships, sex, booze, drugs…you get the idea. Plus when you are living completely in your purpose, you attract the right people for you. We can't completely know you and love you if you don't show us who you really are and start to love that person too.

Here are some questions from my program, The Glow Program, that we ask when working on finding ourselves again:

1. What do I currently *love* doing?
2. What do I love that I am currently not doing?
3. What did I find myself doing most as a child?
4. What energizes me?
5. What makes me forget to eat and pee?
6. What brings me joy?
7. When am I most myself?
8. What comes easy to me?
9. Who or what from my childhood brings back a relaxed, healthy version of me?

When asking yourself these questions, put some good old-fashioned thought into your answers. Some of the answers might come easy to you and some might be hard to face. This is the time when we face them anyway, so grab a pen and start now.

When we begin to remember the things we once dreamt up and found hours of joy in, we might feel a little sad. Like finding a toy in the attic that once was our sidekick and now has been kicked to the side. It's okay. Find the familiarity in these memories and use that to restructure your plan. Does it hurt a little to see the easel that is tucked under years of cobwebs and moving blankets? Is it too much emotion for you to blow off the dust and see where you left off? It's okay.

If you are ever going to put these pieces of you back together, then sooner or later the dust has to be shaken up. It will probably go all over the place. You might even get a little in your eye and get super annoyed and discouraged, but the dust always settles, leaving nothing between you and your dreams. Fresh starts often come with fresh wounds. The bleeding will stop and the scar is what will tell your story.

Nothing makes me sadder than hearing about someone who once was a wonderful baker, French horn player, jazz dancer, florist, numbers gal, corporate powerhouse, etc., but who has put that love on a shelf. Maybe life changed and they had no choice but to go another direction to keep themselves or a family afloat. But somewhere deep down inside of that French horn player, there is a song that is on a loop, continually playing in their soul…a song that will never stop until the music starts again.

So here you are, probably sitting on your couch after your kids have gone to bed and the house is finally quiet. Your phone won't stop buzzing with soccer practice and PTO fundraiser reminders, and you're going to be lucky if you even get to wash your hair in the shower tonight. How in the hell are you supposed to read this book, retain what it says, take the steps, change your way of thinking, build a fairytale life, move to a castle, and find your townspeople when you can't even process doing the dinner dishes?

Well, congratulations, princess, because you have already achieved step one: deciding that you need a change. That's why you bought this book after all, isn't it?

Deciding to take the quantum leap into our past is the first giant step. Making that decision means your mind is now open. You're realizing you can't exactly sit still where you are currently placed. Something isn't fitting anymore. Don't panic. It doesn't mean that you have to change your entire life if you don't want to. It might just mean a small shift is needed, or you might need to move tectonic plates. It all depends on what you want.

When I moved out for the first time at nineteen, I had a handful of belongings. Most fit in a couple of shoeboxes, but my family made sure that I had what I needed to start out with. One of those things was an old hand-me-down couch that pulled out into a bed.

Opening up the seats revealed an old pullout mattress that had a metal bar straight through the middle that would dig into your back every time you slept on it.

Every year around tax time, if I got a tax return, I would have just enough money to buy four items: a new shower curtain, a matching toothbrush/soap dispenser set, a new bathroom rug, and a couch cover. Being able to purchase these things was a very big deal to me then. Especially the couch cover. I would stretch it over the old worn out fabric, and within minutes I would have a brand new look. A flower or striped pattern of navy and burgundy (it was the '90s, y'all) would hide all of the flaws and faded colors of the couch.

But every night I would have to strip back that couch cover and unfold all of the parts to create a bed. Even though that metal bar hurt like hell, it was still a place of comfort. But no matter how many different couch covers I bought over the years, one thing remained the same: the broken-down couch underneath.

Finally one day, I decided I'd had enough of my nightly discomfort. I found a way to fix the metal bar and added some egg foam padding. The padding made it hard for the mattress to fit in the hideaway, and the couch cover no longer fit, but I suddenly didn't mind. I loved that I had fixed that old couch myself and I loved that it had continued to be a familiar place for me to relax. To rest. I no longer had to strip back the cover to reveal the sturdy structure. It just sat there, with all of its faded colors and bumpy seats, inviting all who visited to sit awhile.

We might have a broken metal bar right down the middle of our backs. Our colors might be faded. We might feel broken-down and used. It's easy to throw on that shiny new cover and hide what's underneath, but someday that cover won't fit anymore because the work we have done will no longer allow for it to fit. All that will be left will be us. Sturdy, solid us.

It's time to uncover what is underneath.

Do the work, fix what you can, and accept what you can't. Couch covers never stay put anyhow.

I'll close this chapter with something that will keep you thinking for a while.

I want you to be prepared, because this next part might bring up some emotions that aren't always pretty. Once you start to really remember who you were and what you love, you are going to start taking notice of the people who are already doing those things and it's gonna hurt. You might feel envy or jealousy because you realize there are people who didn't stray too far from who they are, and dammit if you don't feel like it's too late for you now.

Hear me now, loud and clear: it's not too late. It's not, babe. I cross my heart that it's not. Oh, and the envy you're feeling? GOOD! It means that there is some fire left in you. Now don't let it burn you out; let it fuel you to get going. I know firsthand that it might make you feel defeated to see others living your dream life, but do you know what it really means? It means that if someone is out there doing it, then so can you, and don't even get me started on the fear of oversaturation, because I opened a hair salon in a small town where there were fifteen (yes, count them, *fifteen*) other salons and more to come. Over a decade later, we are so busy that we need to hire more team members. There is room for every single one of us because our gifts are all unique and different. Stop getting caught up in why you *can't* and start getting caught up in how you *can*.

One night I was listening to a conversation between world-renowned American chef and restaurateur Thomas Keller and television writer and producer Philip Rosenthal. They were discussing Thomas Keller's heart behind opening his restaurant, Ad Hoc (which literally means "for this purpose"), in Napa Valley and talking about how there was a need for a comfortable place for the community and families to dine. Especially those families of the chefs that run The French Laundry, Thomas's three-star Michelin restaurant.

When Thomas explained to Phil the idea behind Ad

Hoc, Phil matter-of-factly and easily replied, "Oh yes, if you want something, make it." As if he were saying, "Duh, that's what we incredibly super successful entrepreneurs do." No questions asked. No wondering if it's a stupid idea. No worries that it might not work. Just simply, "If you want it, make it."

This got me really excited, and I could feel the energy buzzing inside of me. Why? Because it takes all of the complicated out of "how to make an abundant life for yourself that you're over the top in love with" and simplifies it down to a one-liner that packs more punch than one of Thomas's tasting menus. "If you want it, make it."

Do you see how simple this can be? Find something you want, and make it. Don't allow yourself to get caught up in the "why you can't," and instead, get caught up in the "how you can." Nothing great ever came from second-guessing. Nothing great ever comes from lukewarm maybes. If you want something great, you have to go all in. Your *why* is your want. Keep going back to it. If you want something, make it happen. Build it, create it, dream it up, and take actionable steps toward your goal. Plan it, envision it, love it. (We are going to learn all about this.) Sink yourself in the waters of it and swim like hell. Name it, water it, nurture it, fall for it. All before it's even here. There is nothing like creating something out of nothing that is wonderful and serves yourself and others.

Now get excited because you are on your way!

Chapter 2:

HEY LITTLE CATERPILLAR (SHEDDING YOUR OUTER LAYER) GUIDING YOU TO SHED THE PROTECTIVE COVER THAT SHIELDS THE REAL YOU

I REMEMBER THE FIRST TIME EVER in my life that I became body conscious. I was in the sixth grade, and back then whoever was the oldest in the neighborhood was in charge of all of the other younger kids. I didn't need a babysitter. I was plenty old, in my eyes, to take care of myself. But since that isn't how it worked in 1990, our neighbor (and my makeshift big sister) was put in charge. She was in eighth grade with beautiful blue eyes and was the apple of the eye of the eighth grade boys in town.

It was a warm spring Saturday and as soon as the 'rents left the area, a few of the boys rode up on their huffys and dropped them in the yard. They believed that they were the kings of the town in all of their fourteen-year-old glory. Hormones raging so fiercely that you could actually smell the pheromones wafting off of their skin. Cracking voices and goofy laughs suddenly emerged in the front yard of my house, where my sista from down the block and I were sitting on a blanket, making friendship bracelets. The boys were awkward and dorky, like all of us were at some point in middle school. All but one.

Noah Landry wasn't like the other boys. He had moved to our little town from Louisiana just a few years prior. While the other boys were punching each other in their not yet muscular arms while saying, "Shut up dude!" in high-pitched voices, Noah was intently focused on my neighbor. Noah was a bull rider and had a Cajun accent that was smooth yet edgy. I could tell right away that he was confident, and that made me nervous.

In an attempt to flirt with my neighbor and show off a bit, Noah grabbed a hose that was wound up in my mom's flower garden and threatened to spray us, causing us to run around the yard, screaming and laughing, "Noooooo!"

Suddenly, I felt the ice cold hose water hit me square in the chest, taking my breath away for an instant and leaving me frozen in place while Noah sprayed me down. As the cold water hit my white t-shirt, he laughed, "How old are you?" He smirked. "Girl, you need to wear a bra!" he exclaimed with a little bit of evil in his eye.

He said that. In front of the other boys. In front of another girl. In front of the neighborhood, the county, the universe. That's what it felt like anyway.

I quickly pulled the material of my now see-through shirt away from my cold, clammy body and, with a hot, red face, ran into the house to dry off and die of embarrassment.

I would spend the next 30 years of my life clasping my shirts in front of my body and constantly fidgeting with my clothes to make myself more comfortable.

Now, if you have seen me on stage or have seen photos of me on social media, then you are probably thinking that

I look pretty darn comfortable...but the truth is that the people who are closest to me and the many who have photographed me know.., getting me comfortable on stage or behind a lens has never been an easy task.

It would take me years and years to feel comfortable enough to shed this old wound...and my kimono.

When we talk about shedding the outer protective layer that we have housed ourselves in like a shell for all of these years, it's going to feel uncomfortable. Just like walking outside in a bikini in the middle of January, walking out of your old ways that have been wrapped around you like your Grandma's afghan is going to feel cold, unnatural, and you will feel naked.

We have spent so many years cocooning ourselves in who we have come to believe we are, and here is what has caused this:

1. Society
2. Who everyone else tells us we are
3. Insecurities

This trio takes us on the dance floor and leads the whole time, steering us to the right and then to the left until we are dizzy and out of breath.

Let's start with society.

Maybe you really resonated with making art as a kid, and that love for art followed you into your teen years and eventually adult years. Night after night you came up with a plan of how you would start your career in art and travel the world, discussing the latest hot art show in Paris over café au lait on the Champs-Élysées. You are, in every sense of the word, an artist. But wait...what does society *think* about artists? Ooooh, ooooh, pick me! I am a musician, I can answer this one. Society tells us that being an artist isn't reliable. Sensible. Responsible. Next thing you know, you are trading in that ticket to Paris for a pay stub and a list of things to do while your boss is in Paris. Just when things didn't seem like they could get any worse…

Enter "who everyone else tells us we are"

You start discussing your plans and dreams with your friends and family, but instead of envisioning your "projets de voyages," you are met with quiet uncertainty and shifty eyes.

"Is that a career that is going to make you any money? I mean, is that responsible for a gal your age?" asks Uncle Jack. Always the one who complains about his meal just to get the freebie.

"She's a little eccentric, but she is super nice," says your best friend, while telling her husband's single cousin about you.

"Sorry, ma'am, we have to have a better record of employment to approve this." The banker is letting you down easy after applying for the loan that would fund your first overseas trip to Paris.

So now, instead of "artist," you feel like the irresponsible weirdo broke girl, which leads us straight into—you guessed it! Welcome to the issue of our- insecurities.

Once we have been hit with the insecurity portion of this dance, we're really far off track from where we started. Nothing seems to make sense and you find yourself saying things like, "I don't even know who I am anymore."

And that is because YOU DON'T! You don't recognize the you who had a fearless dream, because you have been replaced by someone else. Someone who society, everyone else, and your insecurities have *told* you to be.

So now what? You have had the aha moment! You are starting to see a little clearer in this fogginess that has set upon you for so long now. How do you start to feel more like you? What does that look like? It's not like there is a class that you can attend at the local junior college, titled "Remembering Who You Are 101." But here are some steps that you can take to start shedding the cocoon around you and reveal your wings.

STEP 1. IDENTIFY WHAT IS MISSING FROM YOUR LIFE.

You feel it; we all have at some point. The vast void of nothingness that can't be filled. No half-price marks, no cute little quote tattoo on your ankle, no CrossFit workout. Nothing seems to fill it. That's when you have to dig deep into your memory bank…past the NKOTB cassettes, past the Love's Baby Soft and Aquanet… Way deep into your memory you will see it. Who you were when you were enjoying the things you loved.

Once you can identify what those things are, how they make you feel, and *who* you are with those things in your life, you can start to feel again. Step 1 is all about feeling again. As mentioned in upcoming Step 5, it might get a little sticky while you're digging up old feelings, but stick with it and follow the guide. It won't let you fall!

STEP 2. TELL YOUR STORY!

Who are you? Where did you come from? What makes you laugh, cry, cringe? You don't have to write a book to tell your story (but I am seriously hoping that you will consider it, because in my opinion, everyone has a book in them), but tell your story to yourself. Remember what it felt like in some of your happiest times. Remember what makes you *feel* the kind of feeling that you can't explain. Remember what makes you sad, and then see if you can tie some passion to that; is there something that was really hard when you were a kid, but now that you are an adult, you have the knowledge to use that tough situation to take action?

Fuel yourself with emotions and be brave enough to explore what those emotions are. We are complex humans and our stories are all unique to us, just like our gifts. There is no right or wrong when you remember. These are *your* memories and your perceptions. Pull all of these memories together (what made you happy, what made you sad, what brings a full belly of fire and passion to your gut) and then remember who you are deep down inside, past all of the surface and taught behaviors.

STEP 3. START DOING THINGS FOR YOU AGAIN.

Take Step 1 and Step 2, blend them all up together like a protein power shake, and use them to fuel Step 3. As you start to remember the things you love that make you feel in addition to what your story is, then and only then can you take tangible steps back into yourself.

Do you feel your most authentic when you are twirling around in a pair of ballet flats, but you haven't pulled them out of your closet in twenty years because it feels silly? Well, I am here to tell you that it's sillier to leave them in the box.

Put them on your feet and dance. Did you just remember that you were the only person in your lunchroom at school who made room at the table for the kids who had nowhere to sit, when the senior football players used their extra seats for their stack of books? (All love for football people—my son was a football player; this is just my memory from high school.) Did that fuel you up a bit with some fiery passion? What can you do right now to sew some of these threads of you back together? Once you identify what makes you tick, the possibilities are endless.

STEP 4. FIND YOUR WHY AND FOCUS EVERY SINGLE FIBER OF FOCUSING THAT YOU HAVE ON IT.

Your why is going to be your core that will help keep you laser-focused and standing upright when things feel like they are jumbled and falling down around you. You can always go back to your why and remember exactly why it is that you started this journey anyhow.

Finding your why is not as complicated as some make it seem. It can be as simple as "I want to teach my daughter that anything is possible," then working toward your goals, remembering when things get hard (and they will) "I am doing this because I want to teach my daughter that anything is possible." Reminding yourself of your why will keep you motivated and on track vs. walking around blind, forgetting why you are putting yourself through all of this and trying to remember why you started in the first place.

STEP 5. CATERPILLARS, GIVE YOURSELF SOME GRACE.

This journey back isn't going to be an easy overnight trip. You may have to pave some of your own roads and carry water on your head, only to have it spill, but every little step forward is a step back to your true self. Be gentle with your soul, give yourself massive amounts of love, understanding, and forgiveness as you start to shed your protective coat. You're going to look back at some of the decisions you made and cringe. Try to remember that these decisions were necessary to form your story. Lessons to carry with you and learn and teach from.

Did you karaoke "Stroke It" after too many shots of tequila at the employee Christmas party? Yes, yes you did. Is it one of your coworkers' favorite stories to tell and you can both belly laugh about it now? Yes, yes you can. We do things in our lives that serve us during that time, and no matter how uncomfortable it is to look back at some of those things, we must remember that we were still just a little caterpillar and not yet a butterfly. If you are really struggling with this I want you to repeat after me: "I did the best I could with the awareness level that I had at the time."

Once you start to practice these steps and unveil what you have always held underneath that tightly gripped t-shirt, you will be ready to take some actionable steps that will launch you into the life you've always dreamed of.

A little note on fear and gut...

During this transition it's important to learn the difference between instinct and anxiety. It is very easy for these two lines to become blurred, and sometimes they can feel like one big ol' stress ball. A few years ago I had an experience that taught me a *huge* lesson between fear and gut... I was heading on a solo trip and had days, if not weeks of anxiety leading up to it. I was frustrated with myself because one of the core things that I teach is that we must get comfortable with the uncomfortable, and I was currently failing miserably.

As I forced myself to pack my luggage, I asked my husband, Terry, "Why can't I just be like those women who can get on a plane and fly off to somewhere they have never been with grace? Why can't I be cool like that?" I was beating myself up. It was really something! Flash forward to arriving on said trip. From the second I landed, I could feel that something was off. Something just wasn't sitting right with me, so I got super brave and left. There were no flights going back to Chicago for three days, so I did what I could do and booked a one-way flight to a city I had never been to. I figured if I could get there, then I would be an hour-and-a-half flight away from home, much closer than my four-and-a-half-hour flight from Mexico.

While I was walking through the airport, I realized something. I *am* that woman who can get on a plane and fly to somewhere she has never been, with grace. I *am* cool like that. You see, the lesson is this: I kept telling myself that I was afraid, when the truth is, I was just very intuitive and in touch with my gut.

While thinking back on what was making me feel all of these feelings exactly, it's hard to pinpoint one thing. What I can tell you is that everything around me made me uncomfortable. Things that normally would have convinced me to stay (like sunny Mexico palm-tree breezes) were replaced with a gray flooded mess. Now, was Mexico really a gray flooded mess? Not really, it had simply rained, but since something bigger than me knew that I wasn't supposed to be there, I was able to see through a different lens. Had it been beautiful, I might have stayed.

Asking to see clarity instead of seeing through rose-colored glasses is a great way to notice what is really happening around you. I use this prayer/mantra every day. Be prepared for what you might see; things aren't always what they seem, but we don't have time for guessing games while we are busy building our new best self!

So, how do you tell the difference?

When I am feeling anxious, I ask a lot of questions to a lot of people. "What should I do? What do you think? Am I just worrying?" But when I feel a gut instinct, I act alone and know that I am making the right decision.

Anxiety causes chaotic thinking, but gut instinct causes clear, centered thinking. When I arrived at the airport to get on the plane to Charlotte, I took a deep cleansing breath and felt centered and certain, not questioning my choice.

Intuition tends to feel *right*. It feels clear, calm, effortless, and smart. Things tend to open up. When my plane landed, my luggage was first out on the turnstyle, and when I approached the ticket counter I was able to easily (and affordably) buy a one-way ticket to Chicago that boarded in two hours, giving me plenty of time to get a bite to eat and even enjoy a coffee.

Anxiety will feel cloudy and scary and confusing. It won't flow. In fact, it will stop the flow. While both anxiety and intuition can create an unsettled feeling, anxiety will likely lead to more uncertainty, while instincts will feel more concrete.

Side note: if you tune into your body and something is screaming *no* to you, act now. Don't try to figure out if it's fear or instinct—you can figure that out later! Run, get yourself to safety, and figure out what the heck was happening later. Most likely it's your gut! GO!

Chapter 3:

WELL THAT'S PRETTY GUTSY (LEAVING A LIFE THAT IS NO LONGER SERVING YOU AND NEVER LOOKING BACK) GUIDING YOU TO PLAN FOR BIG CHANGE

CONGRATULATIONS! YOU HAVE BROKEN THROUGH your cocoon and have peeked your head out into this brand-new world that you will use your new wings to fly through, seeing the world from a whole different view. But wait, you don't yet know how to fly. You don't even know how to flap your wings! How do we prepare for takeoff?

This chapter will help prepare you and guide you for big change.

When my husband and I made our first jump into the entrepreneurial world (a small salon in the historic downtown district of our city), everything was stacked against us. My credit was crap from years of bad money management and a sticky, financially screwed divorce; I had no money and had to ask the bank for a loan but couldn't get one on my own and had to ask my dad to co-sign. I had never owned a business before and I had to renew my cosmetology license because I had let it lapse. I was most certainly in the "ready to use my wings but have no idea how" stage of my journey. But we had made the decision that we were going to make this happen somehow, some way.

I was working a fairly secure job at a hospital but didn't see eye to eye with my manager and was increasingly unhappy at work, but I'd always felt a pull in my heart to do something that would allow my creative gifts to shine. I will be honest, hair isn't my favorite, but it's hair and hair alone that has been by my side through thick and thin (ha...) I *knew* there had to be more than punching in and being ridiculed for being thirty seconds late or being written up for giving a patient a warm blanket from radiology (against policy and procedure to get a blanket from a different department) when she was shaking down to her core after receiving some bad news. There had to be more for me.

When we finally entertained the idea of actually purchasing a business that had come into our path (at exactly the right time...thank you, universe) we had to jump. We realized that there was never going to be a perfect time to yell BINGO, so we just stood up and shouted BINGO! YES!

I wish I could tell you that once we took over the salon, everything was a fairytale, but just as luck would have it, it was not. The first six months were spent bringing customers in the door after the previous owner failed to hold up her end of the bargain and conveniently forgot to mention that someone was taking the reins, leading the customer base to believe that the salon had actually closed. Then nine months in, the entire salon burned down. Some might say that should have been a sign. Some might even say we made a mistake in buying the place, but I believe that we don't change if we're not challenged. So we learned and we grew and we struggled and we grew some more, and now I am proud to have run a successful, beautiful salon with a team who has been with me for over a decade. When you decide to jump, you might sprain your ankle and have to limp along for a bit, but you will have escaped the fire.

God didn't give us our gifts only for us to ignore them, yet so, so many of us do. When we no longer can ignore the feeling, we finally act. Let's call that stage "the pull."

I recently had a nice conversation with a man in our community who is well-respected and one of the best storytellers I have met. He told me the story of a man who died and went to Heaven. When he arrived, St. Peter met him at the pearly gates. St. Peter asked the man if he would like a tour of Heaven, and the man excitedly followed him through the beautiful gates. When the tour was nearing the end, the man noticed a door that was shut tight.

"What does that door lead to?" the man asked.

Shifting his gaze down, the smile slowly faded from St. Peter's face. "There is a very sad room behind that door," he said.

The man, increasingly curious about what could be in the room, asked if St. Peter would let him see the room. St. Peter warned the man again, "This is the saddest room in Heaven. I'll open the door so you can see for yourself." St. Peter opened the door and the man stood silently in awe.

Behind the door were shelves as long and as tall as the eye could see. On the shelves were the most beautifully wrapped boxes. Gold strands of ribbon fell gently around each golden box. The boxes shimmered so brightly that it was almost blinding.

"What is this beautiful room?" asked the man while slowly taking in every detail.

"These, my son, are all of the unused gifts that God has given to humans. The saddest part is, they can't be regifted. They were meant for one person and one person only."

This story stopped me in my ever-loving tracks. Okay, so I wasn't crazy and defiant and unable to work for a boss. I was doing exactly what I felt pulling on me, and that was one of the gifts that I have been given. Hair, although I have been licensed and practicing for twenty-four years, wasn't exactly my gift, but the gift was found in being able to open a business that brings women together. From our salon family to our guests, I strive everyday to encourage, empower, and love big. Having this salon has given me the space to do so. It has also taught me how to run a business in order to open another just a few short years later.

When you are focused on using your gifts to serve yourself and others, you will find that opportunity knocks, and when it comes a-rap, rap, rapping on your door, you'd best be ready to open it.

So how exactly do we plan for this in an unplannable world? A few easy steps can get you ready to live your best life. Planning for making huge giant steps and massive change is much more doable if you view it as planting a few plants at a time vs acres and acres of corn. Breaking down your goals into actionable steps (e.g., milestones, task list, prep work, timeline) will allow you to get really great results much faster than if you just jump in willy-nilly.

STEP 1. ACKNOWLEDGMENT.

Acknowledge the pull. You feel it, you have been thinking about it, and now it's time for you to shake hands and share an appetizer platter with it. Get to really know and understand the reason you want a change. Accept that you are growing and what used to serve you may not anymore, and that is A-OK.

This is the seed planting stage, and although you can't yet see it, that seed is starting to take on a life of its own and grow roots. Kind of like when you start dating someone you think you really like. The most important part of this step is understanding why this change is necessary for your growth. If you ignore the pull, it will only pull harder and harder. You might not be able to tell at first, but soon there will be signs showing up. You may feel uneasy or unsettled and have the constant feeling that something is missing. Things might even appear through physical manifestation. I am a big believer in emotional crud manifesting as physical crud.

If I haven't mentioned it yet, I am a singer songwriter and have been writing since I was a kid. I have also sung in bands since I was twenty. Somewhere along the line I started singing more and more cover songs, and eventually *all* cover songs, and little by little my songwriting was put on the back burner. I felt the pull to write but ignored it or just watered it a tiny bit by picking up a guitar and strumming a few chords and then putting it back down, giving up. I was unmotivated and in a dry spell but not really doing much about it. Flash forward to the age of thirty-three. I was deep into the cover band world and hadn't written, let alone sang any of my own songs. I knew I was using my voice but not using my gift. I felt the pull but again pushed it back down. In September of 2011, three days after my thirty-third birthday, I would undergo a major surgery to remove a rare cancer tumor in my throat, near my vocal cords. I would wake up from surgery cancer free but unable to sing due to some complications with the vocal cords themselves. Terrified, I began the journey to find my voice again. A year later, my voice came back to me after a lot of tears, wine-induced ugly-crying emotional nights, anger, prayer, pleading, doctor appointments, voice coaching, and just pulling a guitar out and trying.

After all the dust settled I looked back on the experience in order to try to understand what I was supposed to learn from it. What came to me so strongly was that I wasn't using my gift the way it was intended to be used (writing music, storytelling, speaking to women, using my story to inspire and motivate), and the universe tried telling me by bringing attention to the one area that I needed to use: my throat. Now, I am not saying that if you ignore the pull, you will suddenly be riddled with disease and horrible luck, but it might be worth paying attention to things happening in your life, your mind, and your body. You might discover a tiny little flicker that is calling to you. The pull is not something that should be ignored. Fan that flicker and see what comes of it.

STEP 2. COMMUNICATION.

Start talking, but not blabbing. This is the time when you'll want to start discussing the pull with those who love and support you and your ideas (not quite everyone yet). This is a great time to start brainstorming with those you love and start getting some energy behind you. For example, maybe your sister is your biggest fan and adores your baking. She might be a good go-to when starting to discuss your thoughts. The script may go a little something like this:

You: "I'm thinking of opening a bakery. You know how much I love to bake, and I really think turning it into a career is part of my path."

Her: "Oh my cupcakes, I never thought you would say this and always hoped you would! I am so excited! What can I do to help?"

A word of warning, from experience of course: be cautious who you share your vision with during this step. This is not the time for nay-sayers and negativity. That will just create fear, and you are making some of the bravest decisions you have ever made right now. We have no room or tolerance for fear and doubt. Only those who you trust fully with your vision should be in the know, and this is why: when others are excited with you, the pull really starts to gather some energy and starts its forward motion!

Sometimes during this stage we start to find our people, and sometimes our people are not who we thought they would be. I have been supported and loved fiercely by people who I had no idea even knew my name, let alone believed in my dreams and goals. I have also been ghosted by those I thought were ride or die. This is similar to when you start getting serious with a new partner. You start meeting new people and new friends, and sometimes your old friends won't dig this. Or they will, and all of a sudden you have this new tribe of people who you never thought would come together. You are starting to plant the seeds for your new journey and if you just keep watering the seed, eventually it will start to grow. This is the "we are Facebook official" stage. One of the most exciting stages because things are starting to gain forward motion. If I could use emojis in this book, I would totally put a cheering emoji right here!

STEP 3. DEVELOPMENT.

Put this bad boy in ink. This is the *really* exciting step! This is when you start laying out some actual tangible plans. This is where you take all of your brainstorming ideas and start whittling them down. Okay, you have decided (and now your sister is holding you to it, because if you don't open a bakery then she will die…just die) that yes, you are doing this! You can no longer just sleep with the Pull after dollar bottle night; it's time to put a ring on it, baby.

Lay it all out, journal, make phone calls, research, journal more, use that little section in your phone titled "Notes," and everywhere you go take notice of what is happening around you. Snap pictures, make goal boards, chunk down your tasks into milestones, start lists, set a timeline. Whatever it is that you can do to make this seedling of an idea sprout, then by golly, you do it.

You might have to put a little heat on it and speed things up, so you pull out your grow lamp and plug 'er in. You might have to get brave and put that deposit down or order some killer business cards. Coin a name or copyright an idea, sign up for the class, book the trip. You get the picture. This is the watering of the sprout stage. The wedding planning stage.

STEP 4. IMPLEMENTING.

It's go time! This is the step when you take all of your data and get hella clear on exactly where you want to be and what you want to do, and then start taking the steps to solidify those wants. You dreamt up your bakery idea, you shared it with a few trusted sources, and you have a great buzz of excitement going on around it. You've researched what you'll need to get started and now it's time to sign on the dotted line. This is the marriage ceremony of you and the new you. This is when you harvest your crop and get ready to feast…but there is still work to be done before we can get to Step 5.

Sometimes this is the step where you'll run into issues. The caterer for your reception doesn't show up. Your second cousin is already drunk. When things really start moving for you, they might start feeling like they're spinning out of control. You may feel like you bit off more than you can chew and that you have zero control over things. This is when you need to remember why you fell in love, planted the seed, and felt the Pull in the first place.

Always go back to your why. *Why* are you planning for these changes? The answer should be: so that I can use my gifts in the greatest capacity possible. Once you remember this, you will be able to let go and allow the universe to do its thing. Congratulations! You have stepped into the new you.

STEP 5. CELEBRATING.

"Celebrate good times, come on!" The most overplayed wedding song of the 80s and '90s should be ringing in your ears right now. You did it! You took the steps that will allow you to make a *massive*impact on the world. By choosing to honor the gifts you have been given, you will be living in sync with exactly who you are and what you were meant to be doing with them. You will start living in a state of gratitude every single day because you will never have felt more aligned with who you are as you do right now. When that first rush of customers come through your bakery door and those first five star reviews show up on Google, it will start to feel real. This is the time to feast on what you planted and allow it to fulfill you. You should be so. Darn. Proud by the time you get to this step. This is your wedding reception. *Clink clink!*

These steps can be used when planning for change, whether it be personal or business. Looking to make huge improvements in your life doesn't just mean "start a company." By all means, if starting a company is in alignment with becoming the best version of you then let's go! If being in alignment with becoming the best version of you means that you are able to be a full-time parent, part-time cat sitter, sometime rock climber, then let's go!

Whatever it is that makes you feel the pull is right for you. The steps are the same to achieving your goal, but everyone's destination is completely different. This, my friends, is what makes the world so colorful and shiny and bright, and this is exactly what you are going to remind yourselves of when things start to happen for you.

Sometimes we start taking the steps and something sidetracks us (ahem… global pandemic, anyone?), and we have to start over. If this happens, it's okay! Think of it like working out. You are hitting the gym on the daily and really getting the hang of it. Maybe you're rockin' that new hot yoga class and feeling the best you have in years, when suddenly you come down with bronchitis and miss a few weeks. Even though you missed a few steps and feel like you went backward a bit, you're still further than you were before you started.

I know from experience how hard this can be on our minds and spirits. You might even feel like you just cannot conjure up the strength to start again. It was hard enough the first time, and now you have to restart your whole plan. Or maybe, if you're like me, you beat yourself up every day because you count how far along you *could* have been, had you not been sidetracked in the first place.

Well, from experience and in the most gentle loving voice, I am telling you that it will do you no good to wallow in this, and it will only delay your new start from, well, starting. Start over as many times as you need to, and allow yourself to have a knowing that it's totally normal and part of the process.

Chapter 4:

DON'T TELL ME WHAT TO DO- BUT TELL ME IT'S OK (LEARNING TO STOP NEEDING APPROVAL FROM OTHERS AND STAYING CONFIDENT WHEN THINGS START TO HAPPEN) GUIDING YOU HOW TO STAY CONFIDENT WHEN THE BIG CHANGE STARTS TO OCCUR

Do you remember when you took swimming lessons as a kid and went to the pool for the first time after you finished your test and passed? Armed with your goggles, sunscreen, and brand-new swimsuit you confidently marched your way up to the high-dive ladder.

"Be careful now, go slow," your dad cautiously warned. You side-eyed him and kept marching forward, up the ladder and to the slick blue board. While you walk to the end of it, you envision yourself launching high into the air before you finally splash down into the cool blue water below. You are a swan! You are an Olympian! You think to yourself, "Don't tell me what to do. I've had the lessons. I know exactly what to do! I am an expert! I am a…" Oh man, this is a lot higher than you remember. You slow your roll. Then you hear your dad again. "It's okay! You can do this. Just jump!"

This scenario isn't much different from jumping into the new you. You have done the work and you are well into the lesson and understanding your purpose, but sometimes you get a little tripped up and need some encouragement. A little push off the high dive, if you will.

I'm sure you are familiar with these phrases:

"It takes a village!"

"Teamwork makes the dream work!"

"There is no 'I' in team!"

Building a team of support around you is hands down, by far the best thing you can do as you run in the race back to you. Do not attempt this alone. Being that one of the best tools in your toolbox is a team, it might sound contradictory when I say that there is a fine line you will have to learn to walk, and that line is…

APPROVAL VS. SUPPORT

The old you needed approval from others. Does this scenario sound familiar?

It's Friday night. You are twenty-three years old. Your best group of girlfriends is at your condo, and the plan is to get ready together before heading out for sushi and drinks. Every light in the house is on and things you didn't even know you owned, like curling irons, makeup mirrors, and red lipstick, are appearing out of thin air. The Sister Hazel Pandora station is playing on someone's phone, and everyone is feeling great. You pull out your favorite little black dress and slip it on.

"Does this look okay?" you ask your crew, as you turn and look at yourself sideways in the mirror. Even though you LOVE this dress and know that you knock it out of the park when you wear it, you still feel the need to get everyone's approval.

"Oh, you look hawwwt!" your friend squeals.

And suddenly you are confident again.

"Wait, no! You always wear black! Here, try this. YES! Blue looks great on you."

But you don't love it. And now you're conflicted. You really really love your little black dress. It's breathable and you can move in it without feeling awkward, but friend #2 is right. You always wear black.

You settle for blue. You spend the rest of your evening tugging at the seams and dreaming about your pajama pants.

Unfortunately, this script doesn't fit the new movie you are starring in because here's the thing: if you ask everyone around you what they think of your new ideas, new parameters, etc., there *will* be some who are uncomfortable with it and you will never gain their approval. There will be some who think they really do have great ideas (blue dress, anyone?), and you might feel weird shutting them down and standing your ground (you really do look amazing in that black dress and you know it).

You are going to have to get comfortable with instinct and trusting yourself. Getting comfortable with the uncomfortable isn't going to be easy, but it will free you to become everything you are capable of becoming.

When someone doesn't understand our vision, it's easy for them to look disapprovingly on it. If something doesn't fit the box of what they believe to be stable and responsible, then they may look at you a little funny and question you, sending you into a tailspin of wondering what in the hell you are actually doing anyway. This gives us the greenlight to go right back to our old ways, and you've come wayyy too far to walk backward now.

There is no easy way to tell you this. You're going to feel awkward and a bit introverted, but while you are busy making plans to kick ass, you're going to have to put on blinders, put in some earplugs, and sport some protective gear. When things start getting loud and other opinions and low energy come hurtling toward you, you'll be armed and ready. You have to be completely, one hundred percent without a doubt committed to your gifts.

Let's look at your gifts in a different way. Let's say that life is a movie and you have been given a character to play. You get to embody your character and it's up to you to win an Oscar. How do you give the absolute best performance with the character you have been given?

First, you will study the character and soak in every single trait and habit your character has. Then you will practice those traits and habits until they become natural. Once you have that down, you will step completely into your character and align everything you do with that character. You have been given a role and your job is to perform that role to the absolute best of your ability, no matter what the audience or your co-stars think of you. In the end, when you give your Oscar-winning performance and are celebrated for being the best in your field, everything will start to make sense.

This is exactly like using your gifts.

You have been given a gift. Your first job is to learn all about it. Do everything you can every single day to get to know your gift inside and out. This might mean training, schooling, studying, making more time to get to know it. It might mean less TV and more reading. Fewer nights out on the town and more staying in to study. Once you really get to know the traits and habits of your gift, it's time to practice. Practice until it's almost perfect and then practice some more.

Side note: it will never be completely perfect. That's why you will continue to practice and learn for the rest of your life, but setting a bar like "perfection" will keep you coming back for more. Soon you will be able to align your life with that gift. You open the business, you teach, coach, lead, volunteer. Whatever your gift and the way you can use your gift to serve others and yourself. Just like an actor, along the way, you will be judged.

I would like you to think of Johnny Depp. Think of the way he embodied Captain Jack Sparrow. Tabloids had a ball: "Johnny Depp Has Gone Too Far!" "Captain Johnny Has Lost Touch With Reality!" Can you see the newspaper spinning onto your doorstep now? It may read, "Kelly has lost her mind! Did you hear she quit her job at the insurance company to start a clothing company? I sure hope her husband has good benefits because she just let go of a great job! What is she thinking? How irresponsible!" But guess what... Johnny Depp has been lauded for his portrayal of Jack Sparrow and has been nominated for over thirty awards. People who called Johnny Depp crazy were first in line to see his movies. Just like Johnny, you will eventually instinctively become an expert at using your gift, and people from around the world will stand in line to be a part of what you are throwing down. Pretty amazing, right?

Keep the naysayers and judgers far, far away from your dreams, but be sure to sell them a ticket to your performance when you put on your show. Your biggest critic can become your biggest fan if you never break face and allow them to penetrate the focus of kick-assery. So walk around a ruffled pirate shirt and give a big ol' Captain Jack Sparrow smile to anyone who looks at you funny.

Approval means that you will only walk out in public in your pirate clothes if people give you reason to believe that it's okay. Support is walking out with people next to you saying, "Excuse us! The most amazing pirate you'll ever see is coming through!"

It's healthy to crave support. It's unhealthy to crave approval.

I still catch myself from time to time mixing up the two. Social media has made it too easy to get the approval we think we need by supplying us with never-ending instant gratification, otherwise known as followers, likes, and thumbs-ups. For example, we post a selfie. It's our new favorite. We angled the phone camera just right. We discovered how to use Instagram filters. We screenshot and crop. We write up a cute caption: "Saturday vibes." No…delete. "Loving my new curtain bangs." No…delete. "Curtain bangs = Saturday vibes." Perf. Okay, annnnd…post.

We put our phones down and hear the notifications start rolling in. *Ding…ding…ding…ding…* One like, seven likes, eighteen likes. We scroll and scroll through the comments. "OMG I love your bangs!" "Purrrr." "My bestie is smokin'!"- "You didn't tell me you cut your bangs! Cute!"

We are immediately rewarded in the form of attention and approval for…not much effort, but suddenly we are filled with the most glorious dopamine release. This begins feeding our craving for approval. Do these words feel good? You bet they do…but so does an addict's first taste of cocaine. Does it create an unhealthy habit that will lead us into troubled waters if we continue craving approval from others? Yes, yes it does.

Support, on the other hand, is authentic and takes some patience. Unlike approval, it's not instant. It takes time to build good, trusting relationships with those who will become your support system. Your team. Those who are enthusiastic about your goals and have the ability to make you feel safe and comfortable to be yourself are the people to surround yourself with. The goal here is to build such a healthy and trusting relationship with your support system that when there is feedback given, it is already known that the feedback is given with empathy, love, and a focus on supporting and guiding you with no question.

Another side note: support does *not* mean having a cheerleader who gives you constant praise. A true supporter will look out for what is best for you and protect you and your ideas fiercely, even if this means pointing out ways that you can improve.

Once you can really get a good handle on who you are looking to for approval vs. support, you'll be able to put the people around you into place who will launch you forward. The great thing about support is this: when it's right it's almost always two-sided. The supporter often becomes the supportee, and you can give back in the most beautiful way.

Supporting each other and the give and take becomes an easy dance that both parties benefit from.

When my band, River Road Trio, wrote and released our song "Freedom Of Love," I knew that it needed a music video to really drive home the message of the lyrics, and I could already see the story playing out in my head. My husband, Terry, and I (did I mention he is my business partner, guitar player, band leader, co-writer, and best friend?) sat down with a video production company. It fizzled out before it even got started. Discouraged, we back-burnered the whole idea and moved on for a bit.

Fast-forward a few months, and Terry is playing a solo show at a wine bar, so I stop by to support him. Randomly there is a guy with a video camera shooting footage for a commercial so I approach him and ask him if he does music videos. His name is Steve Rogers, and ta-da! He does! We have this great conversation, and I feel like I have known him for years. We plan a consultation meeting for the following week and I write down my many visions to bring along. The next week comes quickly, and soon Steve and I are feeling the buzz of energy and excitement about the potential project. As an independent musician, there are no labels or investors involved, which means, you guessed it, everything we do from recording music to video or show production comes out of our own pocket. For this reason, budget always plays a big part in whether or not an idea comes to fruition or if it just stays floating around in dream land.

Because this project was going to be centered around the community and those who change lives, I immediately thought about how we could financially support the project with help from our community members. Steve and I came up with a number needed to fully fund the project and got to work. We gave ourselves a month to campaign and fundraise, and in only just one week, because of our amazing community, our project was fully funded and ready to shoot. Steve, his son Cody, the band, some great friends, and so many volunteers from the community worked tirelessly and finished the "Freedom Of Love" music video in record time. It came together flawlessly and has reached hundreds of thousands of people over the last few years.

Shortly after publishing the video we had the opportunity to go to WGN News Chicago and perform the song live. Naturally, we asked Steve to join us to experience WGN and also shoot some behind-the-scenes footage. On our way into the city Steve mentioned that his wife, Amy, was in charge of an organization called SEA (Self Employment in the Arts). She was going to be leading an upcoming conference at Columbia College in Chicago and was looking for panel experts and round table speakers. SPEAKERS! This was one of the goals I had set for myself the October prior, when I was invited to deliver the keynote speech in Wooster, Ohio for a conference called The Power of Her. That speech made me realize how much I want to speak and empower women and entrepreneurs in the arts. See where this is going?

Of course I gleefully asked Steve to put me in touch with Amy, and she and I hit it off over coffee and muffins. Amy and Steve would eventually turn into our dear friends and we still meet weekly to this day for our weekly motivational meetings around our kitchen table covered in laptops, notebooks, brownies, and laughter. These two amazing humans were strangers to us not so long ago, and now we share our goals, fears, dreams, anxieties, wins, losses, and families with each other. We support each other and give honest opinions that are valued by all. We found our people, our team, our family out of the clear blue sky. This is the kind of thing I'm talking about when I describe finding your crew.

Chapter 5:

ROCK N' ROLL (WHEN YOU ARE ON A ROLL) GUIDING YOU TO CREATE ANYTHING THAT YOU CAN DREAM OF

Have you ever had butterflies in your stomach in response to something amazing that is happening to you? That feeling is all of our happy hormones coming together and throwing a party, and it feels *so* good! When you start following the pull and start living life on purpose, you'll find that these moments of exhilaration get closer and closer together, which then makes you want to create more moments and so on and so on. This is a lesson in the law of attraction. Think good thoughts, feel good feelings. When you start to realize that the biggest change you had to make to live out your purpose was simply to change your mindset, you start to understand that anything you want, you can have. Sounds too good to be true, doesn't it? It's not. It's real and it works.

In this chapter I will teach you everything I know about making your dreams come true, and we will continue to bring good to our lives together, long after you have finished this book and started to live your kick-butt life. We will also be building our toolbox in this chapter, and this is critical for surviving the elements (like when fear starts to rain on your parade).

This is when things are going to start to sound a little woo-woo but stick with me. Sometimes it will feel ridiculous, and that's okay. Laugh at yourself and then *do the work*. You won't be laughing for long when you see how quickly the universe delivers to those who truly believe that good things are coming.

We are going to be talking a lot about things like visualizing, prayer, talking to your spirit guides, meditation, gratitude practice, and affirmations. Those words might all seem unfamiliar right now, but soon you will be practicing these ways and using these tools just as naturally as you brush your teeth on the daily. These support systems and tools are put into place to keep you moving forward and up. Without having support systems in place, you will find yourself without any direction, which can cause frustration and, eventually, a downward spiral that can undo a lot of the work you have already put in.

Before we can start building our toolbox, we have to do some important work. This is the part where we get crystal clear and laser-focused on what our dream lives look like. Down to the kind of socks we are wearing. Getting clear on what you want is the hardest part of the journey. The rest is cake. Here is what I want you to remember when you are whittling it down to the perfect details: you just have to know the *what*. The *how* will come to you in time. The *how* will show up for you. You just need to know *what* it is you want, and the more specific you can be the better.

You have already figured out what your gifts are, now

we are going to get super focused on how to use those gifts to create a life that you are so in love with you actually considered sending it a Valentine's Day gift. Let me give you an example. I knew that I was given the gift of writing. I toyed with the idea of writing poems and started with that. I also knew I loved writing short stories in school, and I love storytelling even more. These are some of the realizations I had, but it wasn't clear enough. I had to keep going.

What kind of poet did I want to be? Could I see myself holed up in a fishing cottage on the coast of Maine with long natural hair, writing poetry and growing potatoes and fishing for my dinner? Nope. That wasn't it. But wait… I could see myself turning those poems into songs and performing under hot stage lights to a crowd of people who were swaying to the music and feeling all of the words as if they were written directly for their hearts. YES, now *that* I could get clear on.

As an author, could I see myself writing fiction or short stories? Who was my audience? What message did I want to put out there? What made me tick? Soon it became clear that I wanted to help women around the world live their best lives with the gifts that they have been given. This is the type of getting clear I am talking about, and it leads nicely right into our first tool (enter clapping emoji here).

Side note: not everyone is going to want to use these tools, and that's okay! If you are set against not believing in prayer or guides, that's okay! If vision boards or speaking words of affirmations out loud makes you cringe, that's okay! You can still be a manifesting factory pumping out one good thing after another. These are simply tools you can use if you choose to. Not everyone uses a food processor to chop veggies; some people prefer chopping by hand. Either way, you end up with the same result: chopped vegetables. It's just a tool that can assist in the process, and it's there if you need it.

TOOL #1: VISUALIZATION

Once I figured out what my gifts were, I started to zero in on how I could see myself using them. I would close my eyes and imagine myself boarding a plane on my first book tour. What the jet engine sounded like, what a first class seat felt like (you must think big and abundant!), what I was wearing, what the hotel room looked like once I arrived, what the city that I was in felt like. Who my team consisted of, what the coffee tasted like, what my schedule looked like, etc. until it looks and feels *so* real that there is no choice but to expect it to happen. Once you get this vision down, repeat, repeat, repeat!

Something important to mention here: visualizing is only successful if it focuses on the process, not just the outcome. That is why it's so important to visualize each step and detail. Next, you must put actionable steps into place that support your vision, otherwise you are just daydreaming. So why not just put goals into place and skip the whole visualization junk? Well, scientists are discovering that the mind can't distinguish between imagination and reality. According to the International Coaching Acadamy's neuroscience and visualization research paper, "If you exercise an idea over and over in your mind, your brain will begin to respond as though the idea was a real-world object. The thalamus (the part of the reality-making process of the brain) makes no distinction between inner and outer realities, and thus any idea, if contemplated long enough, will take on a sense of reality. The concept begins to feel more attainable and real, and this is the first step in motivating other parts of the brain to take deliberate action in the world. When we visualize an action, the same brain regions are stimulated as when we physically perform an action. Your brain is training for actual performances. Thinking of picking up your left hand is, to your brain, the same exact thing as picking up your left hand."

Pretty cool, eh? So while our brains and hearts are on a date and making future plans we can be writing out some actionable steps that launch us forward. I see the plane, the hotel, the stage, the coffee... Okay, great..Now what? Now I start researching, calling, emailing, planning, and booking book events.

Visualization is not only a great tool because there is some nifty science backing it but also because there are so many ways to play around with this tool. Let's break down a few of them and let's start with one of my faves: the almighty vision board. (Darn it, why can't books have sound effects? We need a magical fairy sound effect right now.) Oh vision boards, you pretty little squares of hope. I love to vision or goal board in all of the ways! My latest even features a photoshopped version of Willie Nelson standing next me in anticipation of a long-awaited performance. (Hey, Willie... Call me.)

Vision-boarding can seem overwhelming if you let it, but if you think of it as a simple project, it can be fun and mega productive with hella goals. First, choose what kind of board you want to be your base. You can use just about anything to create your board. A magnetic whiteboard with cute little magnets, a piece of cardboard and some Elmer's glue; you can even use your phone and download apps to create a virtual board. My personal favorite is the whiteboard because I found some hip magnets with words of inspo on them, and I can move things around or add text whenever I want.

Next comes the fun part. Start looking everywhere for things that support your goals and reflect your visions. Let's flash back to 1991. Remember when we used to cut out ads from *Seventeen Magazine*? Same idea, friends, but instead of Claudia Schiffer in Guess jeans, we're looking for anything that sparks our attention and makes our heart flutter. (Eat your heart out, Kirk Cameron, we've got a new love in town, and it's called *our dreams*.) Some ideas of things you can cut out are inspirational quotes that resonate with you, photos of places, people, or things that make your heart pitter-patter, creating some of your own art using an online graphics site like Canva to combine your own words or photos, print, and cut those out. Basically anything that envelops your goals and makes you happy and inspired.

My husband and I have multiple businesses, so we like to break our boards down into sections and pick out one visual for each biz. We also like to pick out some "words of the year" and focus our personal and professional goals around those words. More on this in affirmations!

Most importantly, remember to have fun while building this tool. Grab some scissors and a magazine or hop online and start printing. Don't overthink it and don't worry about who will see it either. This is *your* vision coming to life, and that's all that matters! Another way you can use visualization is just as it sounds: closing your eyes and seeing yourself there is one step, but going way deeper and actually *feeling* what it feels like is what will really get your manifesting juices flowing.

Let's try an exercise. You are visualizing moving to St. Thomas to become a deep-sea fishing guide. You might close your eyes and imagine yourself in St. Thomas, on a boat, guiding fishing tours…but wait…your brain needs much more. Try more of a full story with all the details along the way. You packed the last of your things in chilly Chicago. It's December and there was a snowstorm three days ago, leaving dirty snow pressed up against the sides of the highway. Midway Airport is buzzing with the sound of shuttle buses dropping and picking up passengers, and it smells like diesel. It's so cold you can see your breath. Your heart is beating hard in your chest as you throw your checked baggage onto the scale and say a silent prayer that it finds you on the other side of your flight. Security is busy. It's a Friday night after all, and people are rushing to get home from work trips and leaving for short weekend getaways. You finally get through security and buy an overpriced latte just to give yourself a jolt of caffeine. You find your gate and board your plane. The slamming of the overhead compartments finally hush and your plane taxis and takes off. You see the skyline disappear into the clouds and lean your head back to drift off for the remaining four and half hours.

You wake to the sound of the pilot alerting the flight attendants to prepare for landing. Landing is smooth, and as you exit the aircraft, a wall of warm tropical air hits you directly in the face. Even though it is late at night, the smell of grilled meat and Caribbean spices wafts through the air and your stomach rumbles. The latte in Chicago seems like it was ages ago. You climb in a taxi and give the driver the address of where you will be staying for the next two weeks until you're able to move into your new residence. You arrive and are greeted by a bright and cheery Virgin Islander who checks you in and gleefully hands you your key. You find your way to your room, splash your face with water, eat some sweet mango that was in a welcome basket on the bed, and drift off to sleep. You wake up to the sunrise splattering hues of hot pinks and oranges across the white tile floor, and as you pull back the curtains of the glass balcony door, revealing the cobalt and turquoise waves of the Caribbean gently rolling onto the white sand, it hits you. You are a deep-sea fishing guide. YOU are here. THIS is what it feels like. THIS is how you visualize. Welcome aboard!

TOOL #2 PRAYER

Praying is personal, and I actually thought long and hard about how I would address it in this chapter. I am aware and supportive of those who believe in something different, and I want to be sure to state that up front.

The definition of prayer is a solemn request for help or expression of thanks addressed to God or an object of worship. Whether you pray to God or to your dog statue in the front yard, verbally asking for help, guidance, and direction, and then practicing thankfulness and gratitude is powerful stuff. When we succumb to the idea that we are not, in fact, in charge, we let go and let God (or fido...you get it).

I believe that there is something so much bigger than

us in control, and the sooner we learn to let go and buckle up for the ride, the sooner we will be put on the pathways meant for us. Just as with vision boards, simply cutting out pictures and then giving up control while you sit on the couch eating mini Kit Kats out of the halloween candy, waiting for some kind of lightning strike of success, isn't going to cut it. There is still work to be done with prayer. God/he universe is working on your life and you need to partner up, show up in uniform, and be ready to get to it. Just like any kind of work, things go faster and are more doable when there are two people working together as a team.

Prayer seems to come naturally to some, while others don't have the first idea of how to even begin talking to someone or something that may or may not even be there. The entire idea takes faith in whatever you believe, and really, what do you have to lose? I am not a teacher of faith, but I can share with you what works for me and you can take that and make it your own. Creating a habit of praying is a great start and, just as with visualization, will become more and more natural as time goes on. Some people like to find a quiet setting in which they can pray, and some (like me) can pray anywhere. The bottom line is you can pray in any way that's comfortable for you.

When I was young and desperately in need of direction I prayed the same prayer every single night. "Please put me on the path I am supposed to be on. Provide me with guidance because I don't know." It was as simple as that for me. I am going to share something pretty personal with you right now: my current prayer. As much as I possibly can throughout the day, I request one thing over and over.

I pray that "I am placed in front of the people who need me and my gifts, and that the people I need are placed in front of me." I basically give thanks and gratitude for all I've been blessed with, ask to be connected to those who I am supposed to be connected to, offer a whole bushel more of thanks, praise, and gratitude, and finally a hearty amen. I have connected to the deepest, most spiritual side of me and the universe.

I understand and respect that some religions require a much more formal method of prayer; however you are comfortable praying will be the best way.

Next, start the convo. Again, however it is comfortable for you. Personally, believe it or not, I get super shy when praying out loud. There is no right or wrong way to pray. You can think it, sing it, say it out loud, write it, etc. You can have a conversation or recite something memorized. It is honestly one of the most custom tools we have available to us!

Finally, end your prayer. You'll know when your prayer is complete. Remove yourself, still reflectively, from your position or location and go about your day. Easy peasy lemon squeezy.

TOOL #3 TALKING TO YOUR SPIRIT GUIDES

(stay with me, friends. This is a super amazing
tool if you allow yourself to open up to it.)

Archangels, guardian angels, departed loved ones, saints, helpers. No matter what resonates with you, our guides are here and around us and ready to help. They are simply waiting in the wings (see what I did there?), just tapping their foot in anticipation of *you* asking them for guidance!

So what are spirit guides anyway? First off, the idea of spirit guides isn't a new idea. It is a belief that many cultures and religions adopt. Each culture or religion may call guides different names, but across the board they are very similar. Have you ever felt like someone was watching over you? Not in a creepy, horror-movie way, but in a comforting and loving way? Have you ever felt a gentle pull of direction or found a quarter lying on the ground and just knew it was a sign for you? These are the faint whispers from our spirit guides. This may come to you in the form of intuition or simply knowing.

We can start asking our guides for guidance, but be sure to first always ask for protection and invite only the highest of energy and purest guides. This way you will be protected from any tricky business, and it will assure that only the holiest and purest energy is coming your way. Then simply start asking questions. Spirit guides often show up and will enter your life by sending you a sign. Be open and look for the signs, and believe me, they will be there. Have you ever been going through something and the perfect book or song just seems to land in your lap? Some believe it's a coincidence, but I believe there is something deeper. You can even ask for a specific sign like a special flower or a bird or even a word, and watch as those signs start showing up in your life. This is confirmation that you are surrounded by spirit guides who love and hear you!

Calling on your spirit guide is a practice that I use every day. Imagine having a team of people around you who love you *so* much and want only the best results for you. These are pure-hearted people who have no ill will toward you, and you can trust them fully and purely. Now imagine that this team *knows* things that you don't and can send you clues that you are going in the right direction or send you clues (enter gut instinct) that you are not. Well, I am happy to tell you that you have this custom-built team available to you right now, and they are just waiting for you to invite them onboard.

We are going to add a key word here that we will be using throughout the remainder of this book: vibration. You have heard it before and probably have even used it or have hung a cute little Hobby Lobby sign in your bathroom stating "Good Vibes Only," tucked under a painting of a pastel rainbow. Vibrations (vibes) is based on the idea that all matter in the universe is made up of energy that vibrates. The higher the vibration, the happier and more in tune we are with ourselves. The lower the vibration, the heavier, darker, and more confusing things feel. When we raise our vibration by taking part in things like meditation, yoga, breathing exercises, walking in nature, etc., we become closer to our guides, which means we can get clearer signs and messages *so* much easier. Basically, staying in touch with your happiest, most focused self by practicing self-care techniques will attract all that the universe has in store for you.

TOOL #4 MEDITATION

I want to start this section by saying that I am not very good at meditation. So why would I be willing to write about it and guide readers in any way if I am not good at something? Well, simply, this: we are all students in something. Some of us are teachers, yet we are all still students. Just like with exercise, I think it is important to just start. You don't have to be the best Zumba dancer to start Zumba, just like you don't have to be a master of meditation to make it count. I want to introduce you to the idea of getting really still in your mind, allowing space to learn and grow.

All of this to say, I think growth starts by trying things and being really darn bad at them before we are really darn good at them. Think of it this way: you will only be a beginner once. Meditation is all about being in the now, and that is a powerful tool to learn when we have spent years learning to worry about the future and dwell on the past.

My father is a retired financial planner. He made his living helping people plan for the future. Now, let me just state that I believe that planning for the future is definitely important, but I think what we get so caught up in is *worrying* about the future that we forget to live in the moment. Becoming one with your mind and body and letting the stress of the day or moment melt away for a few minutes is incredibly healthy for our mind, body, and spirit.

All of those questions you have been throwing out to the universe, asking your spirit guides and praying about, will have answers to them and when the mind is quiet we can actually hear the answers to what we have been asking. Pretty cool, eh? So, how? How do you start to learn about this incredible tool? For me it was just by jumping in. There are hundreds of great meditation tools online and even on our streaming services, but here are some easy beginner steps to start with:

1. Find some relaxing music, a guided meditation video, or audio and throw your earbuds in. If you

prefer quiet you can absolutely just be—but make sure that any distractions are limited. (Even when using earbuds, be sure to put your phone on Do Not Disturb so that those daily emails that are coming in don't jolt you from your peaceful state of mind.) Some people prefer mantras, and that is a great way to relax and center as well.

2. Find a comfortable place to sit. I actually love sitting on the floor because I feel more grounded there, but anyplace you're comfortable works.

3. Set a time limit. Start with twenty minutes and build up from there. Setting a time limit helps to clear your mind of thinking about how long you should meditate or have been meditating. The last thing you want to do is focus so much on time that you miss the boat all together.

4. Breathing. This is the key to really getting in a good space and becoming aware of your body. Becoming aware of your breath will center you and slow down your thoughts. Focus on breathing in the light and breathing out heavy. There are many articles on breathwork alone that can be found online and will be of great help while learning about meditation.

5. Acknowledge your body. Start to relax your body by focusing on each body part and sending love and good energy to it. Feel the weight lighten as you relax from your toes to the tippy top of your head.

6. This one is where I struggle the most and am still learning. Quiet your mind. This step takes a ton

of practice and mastery, so be kind to your mind, as it will wander. If you notice your mind starts to wander, try to acknowledge it and let it go. Focus on the music or on your mantra. Let thoughts come and then let them go.

7. Once you have completely relaxed your mind and body, you can start listening for answers.
8. After about twenty minutes go ahead and start gently coming back to your center. Wake yourself up a bit if you have really achieved a zoned out, relaxed state. Finish up with a thank you and a grateful heart. You can even put your hands in a prayer position to your heart or your forehead and whisper, "Namaste," which means, "Greetings to you," sort of a thank you/goodbye to your inner self.

Ta-da! You just completed your first meditation!

TOOL #5 GRATITUDE PRACTICE

Oooooh this is my favorite tool! Living with a grateful heart in a grateful life creates more abundance to be grateful for, and this positive way of living is like a magnet for greatness! The coolest part? All it takes is a mindset shift to start. No fancy training, simply changing the way you think. When we live in a state of gratitude we are telling the universe how thankful we are for everything that we are and have. This, in turn, makes the universe very happy, because who doesn't love to be thanked up one side and down the other? What happens when someone is happy due to acknowledgement? You got it. It makes them want to do more good things. This is no different for the universe. When we send out good, happy, thankful, gratitude-filled vibes, they will then bounce back to us. BOOMERANG!

"Well, Jonelle," you may be saying, "this all sounds great, but *how* do we change our mindset to see the good in everything and overflow with joy and gratitude when things feel dark and hopeless and hard?"

I'm glad you asked. If this practice was for everyone, it would be easy, and it's not. Like anything else, it's going to take practice and training. You wouldn't just jump right into a bodybuilding competition without learning and training, but just like starting to add push-ups to your daily schedule, it will eventually become second nature, and that is when you will start to really feel the flow of greatness. Let's go over a few simple ways to dive into this powerful tool of awesomeness.

I want to do an activity with you. Grab a piece of paper or the Notes section of your phone. Now I want you to start looking around your house. What do you see first? Is it dishes that are piled up in the sink or that white trim you thought was going to be so sleek but is now chipped up and in need of a good dusting? Good. You are on the right track. Start noticing the clutter or the extra magazines or the fridge that desperately needs to be cleaned out. Start thinking of your basement and all of the boxes of stuff that you need to sort through. (Stressed yet? Just trust me…) How about that stack of bills that just showed up in yesterday's mail? Okay, you get the point.

Now I want you to shift your mind. Here we go. Get that pen and paper ready. Write down every single thing that comes to mind, but this time put a positive spin on it. "I own so many dishes that I don't even have room in my sink for another mug or spoon. I have beautiful white trim that needs to be wiped off but makes my home look like something out of an HGTV show. I have so many items that there's not even enough room to store them. I have more entertainment than I even have time to enjoy with all of these magazines. I have so much food that we couldn't even eat it all. I have boxes and boxes of memories made that bring me joy. I have bills, which means I have electricity at my fingertips and it will never run out. I also have money in the bank set aside to pay for all of these luxuries." See where I'm going with this? Now start writing down the things that seem small but add up. "We have rolls and rolls of toilet paper, paper towels, paper plates, extra toothpaste, so many socks and underwear we will never be able to wear them all. Shoes literally falling out of my closet, closets full of winter coats, hats, gloves. Lawn mowers, pools, grills, wine glasses, candles, decorations, pets, cars, etc." Keep writing until you are *so* full of gratitude for the things that you have, that you are overwhelmed. Now remember that these items are just the tip of the iceberg because they are just the *physical* things you have. It's time to start listing the other things: friends, family, coworkers, a job, plans for summer vacation, access to great health care. Keep writing until you blow your own mind. I do this regularly and it is a great tool to start shifting the way you think.

Trying to find the positive in every situation is also a great tool. Buyer beware—there will be some negative nannies who will think you are "so annoying" with your brand-spankin'-new positive attitude, but that's because they are living in a negative space, which many times comes from insecurity. The best way to deal with this is to detach yourself. Don't allow their negativity to penetrate your positivity. There will be some people who you love dearly and/or you have no choice but to be around daily who are joy suckers. The best way to keep your energy buzzing and light when around the lower energy and darkness is not to engage too deeply with their negative thoughts.

For example, if someone is constantly complaining and you have tried everything to help them see the positive side of things and they just refuse to shift their mind, you can start to respond with simple things like, "I'm sorry to hear that," or, "Oh gosh, sorry, that sounds tough." This is not a trick for when you are in an actual meaningful conversation with someone going through a hard time, it's just a quick reply for a constant complainer.

Okay, so let's carry on. Back to finding the positive in every situation. You are stuck in traffic. It's freakin' hot. The truck in front of you is blowing off diesel like there's no tomorrow. How…*how* do you find the positive in this? Start by turning on some music and maybe saying a quick thank you for whatever this holdup is for. We aren't supposed to understand it, but I always like to think that there was a reason for the traffic and make the most of it.

From here you just copy and paste. Finding the positive side of the world will leave you feeling so much lighter and free. Remember, this is real life, not an Instagram reel, so there will be days and situations that are hard and just plain suck. It's okay, normal and healthy to not always be happy-go-lucky, but learning how to search for the good vs. the bad is not a bad habit to get into.

While honing these talents, be aware of toxic positivity, a buzzword you may hear. The definition of toxic positivity is dismissing negative emotions and responding to distress with false reassurances instead of empathy. It comes from feeling uncomfortable with negative emotions and is often well-intended but can cause a feeling of disconnection. Some examples of toxic positivity are sayings like "Just keep smiling" vs. "It's okay to be upset," or "It could be worse" vs. "How can I support you?" One of the things I love most is reminding ourselves and others that it's not always easy to see the good in the situation but that we can make sense of it when we can.

So if making a positive shift is our goal but being too positive isn't realistic, and if acknowledging negative emotions is healthy, then what do we do to master our mindset? Well, acknowledging the negative emotion is step one, but learning to let go of it and let it flow in and then flow away is key. Focusing on negative thoughts is where this training will come in handy, helping you break the cycle by becoming aware and then shifting your focus to a positive mindset.

Side note: if all else fails, laugh. Laugh at the irony, the stress, the experience of all of the craziness that is leading you on this new journey. If you feel like crying, which I feel like doing a lot, find something that makes you laugh. Laughing at yourself is one bold way to love yourself fully, and laughing can actually boost dopamine, serotonin, and endorphins, all great supporters of your new positive mindset! Let's go!

TOOL #6 AFFIRMATIONS

*"I'm good enough, I'm smart enough,
and doggone it, people like me."*
— Stuart Smalley

Remember when we all got a kick out of good old Stewie? I know that I used to walk around during sophomore year, laughing with my friends at silly positive affirmations that they loved to mock on *Saturday Night Live*. Remember Chris Farley's motivational speech? Well, we might not all be living in a van down by the river and we might not be standing in front of our bathroom mirrors giving ourselves a pep talk, but my question to you is, why aren't we? Okay, maybe not living in a van down by the river, but why aren't we looking at ourselves in the mirror, right in the eye, and giving ourselves the support we so desperately need to kick ass? Is it because we feel cringy? We were taught that this kind of self-love is dorky, like Stuart Smalley? Is it because we are uncomfortable with believing in ourselves and don't want to be perceived as egotistical and self-absorbed?

Whatever the reason, it's stopping you from achieving your highest self-worth because it's stunting your growth. Remember, to GLOW we must have growth, love, opportunity, and worth, and if we're going to achieve those, we'd better start having some pretty serious one-on-ones with ourselves. One of the ways to start this chat is with affirmations. Affirmations are simply positive statements that are repeated daily, or more often if desired, that will eventually help to make positive changes. An affirmation is defined as "emotional support or encouragement," and research suggests affirmations work in part because affirming yourself activates your brain's reward system, rewiring the brain and programming your mind to believe a specific stated concept. Pretty cool, huh? Yet another magical wand that is already in our hand, just waiting for us to wave it.

So how do you start this wizard sorcery magical action? Well, first, start talking. Write out or find some daily affirmations that resonate with you, speak them aloud (you don't have to do the Stu and talk to yourself in the mirror, but you can if you want, as there is some power in that too), and repeat at least daily. It might feel awkward or weird at first, but it will soon become second nature, and when you start seeing results show up, well, it won't seem so crazy then!

Some simple starters might sound like this:

"I am successful."

"I am confident."

"I am powerful."

"I am strong."

"I am a magnet for good."

"I am abundant."

"I am unstoppable."

And doggone it…people like me.

You can affirm anything that you would like. This is your script. Your customized content. You decide what you want to be available to you and bring that bad boy into reality. The affirmation train is pulling into the manifestation station, and guess what? You are the conductor. Woot woot!

Now that you have some tools in your toolbox, I am going to ask you to get really serious about this whole life-changing stuff. Practice applying each of these tools in your everyday life and watch the magic unfold. Here's the really freaking exciting part: anything that is out there can be yours. If someone else did it, so can you. Let that inspire you and give you energy, not scare you!

Just believe, my sweet monarchs, and watch yourselves transition from that cocooned caterpillar into the beautiful butterfly that lies inside of you!

Chapter 6:

CAN I GET A SELFIE WITH YOU? (AND OTHER WAYS THAT PEOPLE WILL WANT TO LEARN ALL OF YOUR WAYS) GUIDING YOU HOW TO TEACH OTHER TO CONTINUE THE FLOW OF AWESOMENESS

Do you know what's even better than living your best life? Showing others that they can too and watching the flow of awesomeness just continue to…well…flow. Just like being thankful to the universe will in turn make the universe want to give us more, the more we spread love and show others the way, the more we will get back. I lead my business and personal life with one goal in mind: to serve. There are two questions I ask myself daily:

1. *How can I use my gifts to serve?*
2. *How can I lead others to do the same?*

I want you to really ponder these questions and see what answers come to you.

Have you ever had an experience at a new restaurant

and you just can't wait to share with everyone what you have discovered? The feeling of experiencing something amazing and then sharing with others is a big part of the growth mindset. Understanding that there is enough for everyone and that, by sharing, we are expanding energy is a freeing lesson. Once we can adopt this way of thinking, then we are able to take a big cleansing breath, knowing that sharing our knowledge is safe, powerful, and leads to—you guessed it—more abundance!

When it comes to using your gifts to serve others, remember that it doesn't mean that you have to give away your hard-earned lessons and expertise for free *all* the time. There is definitely a time and a place for volunteer work, and we'll touch on that later, but creating income around your knowledge is one of the best ways to fill others' cups while not emptying your own. I am also a *huge* fan of the barter system and feel like this is one of the best ways to share each others' gifts and talents.

Depending on what you're doing in your new and improved life, you can find creative ways to share the wealth. Did you recently become an expert at fundraising? Share a cup of coffee with the person in charge at your downtown development organization and offer your services to them. Think about where you can be of service, find out if there is a need (by asking and sharing an honest conversation), and then offering your services. Be prepared with some information, like an outline of what you do (be crystal clear on what you do—remember, most of the time these are very unconventional talents, and until people know they're available, they may not have ever thought about the fact that they exist), what the expected results are, and price point.

Many times people, companies, and organizations have a need but have no idea where to find the people who fill that niche little corner. This will benefit others and you because suddenly you're doing what you love while doing important work and getting paid what you're worth, which builds your resume and creates more steam behind the train…and off you go!

I believe that it is equally important to give back. If you can use your talents/gifts/services to benefit others with no expectations of anything in return, it's the ultimate thank you to the universe for unveiling your best self. Decide at the beginning of the year what type of service work and how much of it you can donate and stay within those parameters. I have never been disappointed or have regretted donating my talent. It creates such eel-good energy in those around you and almost always leads to more opportunities as the universe once again says, "You are doing exactly what you're supposed to be doing with these gifts! Well done! Here is a prize for you—more opportunities!" It creates a win-win situation; the recipient is grateful, you are grateful, and the universe is one big happy smiley place.

But before you can get there, finding ways to use your gifts is going to take some creative thinking and a lot of shushing your inner critic.

Let's discuss the meat and potatoes of the *how*. I don't want you to get too hung up on the how because sometimes we don't see the how and just need to focus on the why; the how will magically appear. Confused yet? Trust me, this is where the faith part of your journey is going to come in real handy. Trust that it is so and that it is coming, and be open to all of the goodness that flows your way.

The best way I built my creative thinking muscle is to simply start paying attention. Look around your everyday life. Is there something that you're missing? Do you hear others talking about what's missing? Is it something that you know how to do? Boom…opportunity. Once you start tuning in to what is and isn't happening around you, you might be surprised to see how many opportunities there actually are, and even more surprising, how you are the right person to fill the need.

The other way you can figure out the how is by asking questions in your community and/or online, researching what is available, and start from there. So many great ideas and opportunities come from finding a need and meeting that need creatively.

It's obvious that many great businesses can be launched using these methods and this is where my mind always goes first because I can't think of anything better than making a living doing what I love, but what if opening a business isn't what's on your heart? There are a gazillion ways to use your gifts and not have to roll it into a biz plan. You can volunteer, sit on a board, join support groups or lead support groups, tutor or teach online or at a local school… Basically any need that you see could be met with your expertise is going to be a dandy little fit.

A word about finding opportunities to use your talents to serve others. No matter how small, if there is a need, see if you can fill it. Many times these little tests come to us and lead us to bigger things. Remember to protect your energy by taking care of yourself and learning when to lean in and when to lean out. If something feels icky and the energy around something doesn't feel like a positive environment, it's okay to lean out and search for other places to put your energy and your very special gifts.

Now let's talk a little about that inner critic you're going to need to shush. Oh and believe me, you will need to quiet that bad boy up if you are going to take the next step confidently. I remember when I realized that I knew more about booking entertainment and event planning than I ever really wanted to know. After decades of booking two of my own bands, working with event planners, brides to be, school fundraiser committees, so many bar owners that I can't even count them all, and seeing what works and what doesn't when having live music in your venue or function, I found myself with a solid knowledge of how to make a bar a *bunch* of money on entertainment and how to create a seamless, well-attended event by sharing what I have learned on and off stage. I packaged this all up into a pretty little package complete with my "about me" and all of my experience, asked to have coffee with the city planner, and found that yes, they did, in fact, need some direction.

That meeting also led me to a job interview at a college for an entrepreneurial program position that was being created. I threw on a suit, some animal print booties (can't stray too far away from who you really are), and walked tall into the interview. When I was suddenly surrounded by the walls of the school, my inner critic started talking to me. "Ha! You didn't even go to college. How are you going to *work* at a college!" and "You thought this was such a great idea, but you have no clue what you're doing! It's going to show!"

I wish this story had a fairytale ending, but the truth is, I let those voices win that day. The man that I interviewed with was very interested in my knowledge, and when I saw that the position required a minimum of a bachelor's degree, I counted myself out long before he did. He wasn't worried about that requirement. He was confident that we could work around it since I had such vast experience working in the field. But it was too late. I basically talked him out of considering me as a candidate, and when the "thank you, but we have moved on to other candidates" email appeared in my inbox, I wasn't surprised at all. It wasn't because I wasn't qualified, it was because I *told* myself that I wasn't qualified, and that showed up all over my face, my tone, my attitude.

This, my friends, is called imposter syndrome, and she's a biotch. When you start living your brand-new life as your brand-new self, well…she's going to try to come along and really mess things up for you. I picture her as the leader of the popular clique in high school, walking down the hall with her groupies behind her, heading your way and pushing you right into the lockers when she passes you by. Knocking you off track, leaving you feeling embarrassed and flushed and wanting to disappear. Yep…that's her.

Imposter syndrome is exactly what it sounds like: the persistent inability to believe that one's success is deserved or has been legitimately achieved as a result of one's own efforts or skills. It is the explanation of doubting your abilities and feeling like a complete and total fraud. Which, may I remind you, you are NOT.

So let's figure out how to get over this already so that we can get on with the kick butt stuff that you have to do.

Ahem... That *we* have to do. Because y'all, we are in this together!

1. **Stop comparing yourself to others.** You are wasting your precious time, and it's not doing you any good. We live in a world of filters, and social media is soooo yucky sometimes. What we see is not always what we should believe. I personally had to stop following some of the influencers that I was initially inspired by because they were making me sad and less than vs. motivated. They weren't trying to make me feel that way, but I was always feeling one step behind, and that isn't a healthy role model. You are only in the race against yourself, and the only person who you should be comparing yourself with is who you were yesterday.

2. **Focus on your strengths, not your weaknesses.** If I made a list right now of all the things that I can't do, it would be extensive. (Starting with "keeping plants alive.") It would be really discouraging, and ultimately I would start to feel like I was drowning in the "can't" instead of listing all of the amazing things I *can* do. My can-do list is going to be shorter than my can't-do list because there are *many* things that I can't do...but of the things that I can do, I can do them well, and chances are they're the same things on someone else's can't-do list. This is why we need all of the spokes to make the wheel, and my personal favorite quote, "We can't sing harmony if everyone sings the same note." BOOM. You are going to be launching into this new life

with wings wide open, ready to fly, and you'd best be telling yourself that you have superpowers that are yours and yours only. Start making a list of all of the things that you are good at, and when you start to doubt yourself, look at your list and remember who the heck you are!

3. **Use the visualization hack.** Earlier we talked about visualization, and this is an excellent place to use that tool. You have to believe that you are your best version (more on this in the Start Acting step), but even more than going about your day stepping into the shoes of your future self, you need to *see* it. Close your eyes and picture yourself accepting the raise, signing the lease, shaking the hand of the record label president to seal the deal. You have to visualize yourself doing all of the things, but it doesn't stop there. If you want to really see where you are going, then you have to visualize yourself doing the work, taking the steps, getting your hands dirty, withdrawing the last hundred dollars out of your account to pay for your business license. It's way easier to swallow if you can chunk down your steps and visualize each of them as you go. The mountain won't seem so daunting and you'll be hot stepping into your best life!

4. **Understand that failure isn't failing, it's learning.** So here's the thing. You can look at "failing" one of two ways. You can look at it as a set back or a step up. I believe that we don't make mistakes, just steps forward. Even when it feels like we are

going backward. In 2012, just nine short months after I opened my first brick-and-mortar business, a boutique hair studio in the historic downtown district of the city where I was living, it caught on fire and burned down. All that was left standing was the bricks and one wall clock (which we still have hanging there today). We had just taken out a business loan not even a year ago and already had struggled with getting the business off the ground after a business deal went south. This could have, and in all sensible ways probably should have, been a sign to hang it up and walk away but instead of looking at the fire as the ultimate failure in my business, I chose to look at it as a fresh, brand-new start.

Insurance started kicking in, and we were suddenly able to install brand-new stations, shampoo bowls, furniture, and more. We were able to shoo away the old heaviness of the previous owner and create a bright, happy, calm, zen space where men and women alike announce daily upon their visits, "It's *so* relaxing in here!"

Perspective is everything, and if you can see the lesson within the ashes, then you will always be able to let things flow in and out, knowing that if it's meant for you it will be, and growing exponentially since you won't be getting hung up in the "woe is me" parts of growth. Basically, instead of thinking as an imposter—"who do you think you are owning a business?" and all that jazzI was able to say, "I am a strong, smart, business-savvy woman who has taken the bad and created so much good"…and all that jazz.

5. **Talk about it.** Talking about your experiences and hearing how others might feel the same way or have felt the same way helps to normalize these feelings. You are not alone. We're all just trying to figure it out. Yes, all of us! Have you ever seen someone famous, say, in a grocery store, doing everyday things? Did it ever occur to you that they, too, need bread and that they may have even had to run to the bathroom to pee because they drank their venti cold brew just a little too fast? We are all just trying to do our best, and when we start to realize that, it makes us feel understood and accepted. We don't feel like we are running this crazy race alone, and we feel supported, which goes *such* a long way when we are unsure of ourselves.

6. **Start acting.** Act like the person you want to become hint, hint… she is you). Do things like dress for the job you want, not the job you have. Remember what inspires you and add those things to your day. Use your visualization tools to catch a glimpse of who you are at your very best and start doing those things now. Are you healthy and in shape? Are you well-respected and proud of your accomplishments? Start walking in those shoes now and see what unfolds.

Side note: I am not saying to be someone you're not. No, no…that is not allowed here. But what I *am* saying is that you should rise up and be the best version of yourself that you can possibly be in that moment and run with it. Heels, barefoot, work boots, cowboy boots, sandals. Run in whatever you want…just run!

7. **Clap for yourself.** Remember the accomplishments that you have already checked off of your list and celebrate yourself a little. I am guilty of struggling when it comes to #7. My mind is on such a fast track that by the time I accomplish a goal, I am already planning three steps ahead. Although it's great to have ambition and drive, if you don't stop to acknowledge your wins, it can end up being toxic and leave you with your world crashing down around you.

Let me share this story with you. I was sitting in a tiny exam room, waiting to see my family doctor. My doc is pure honey. He is the sweetest, most calm person I have ever met. We share stories about our families and have even challenged each other to do more meditation. He listens and checks on me personally when we are tackling a health issue. He doesn't just treat the body but the heart, mind, and spirit as well. About ten minutes into this particular visit, which was scheduled because my anxiety seemed off the charts and I promised him and myself that I would stay vigilant about mental health, he sat down and looked me directly in the eye and said, "You aren't giving yourself enough credit. You are highly determined and tenacious, and those are great things, but sometimes you need to slow down and remember your accomplishments. Think of all of the great things you have done, you are a great mom with great kids, an awesome wife, an author, you have a great music career and successful businesses. Give yourself some time to enjoy your wins and rest for a bit." By this time I was in a puddle of grateful tears because, for one, that was *so* nice, and this guy was speaking my growth language for sure…and he was right. I have hardly stopped to look around and see what my hard work has brought to me.

Imagine constantly cooking a meal, chopping, steaming, rolling, cutting, mixing, and baking, and pulling it out of the oven never to be looked at again. It's just sitting there, getting cold because you have already begun to chop, steam, roll, cut, mix, and bake again… and over and over and over we go. YES, you are going to burn out if you don't stop to savor your hard work and delicious meal! YES, you are going to be tired and anxious and stressed due to living with unhealthy levels of cortisol ALL. THE. TIME. So remember to give yourself a break. A pause. A hot minute. Can you imagine living a life where no one ever says thank you or shows any appreciation? This is what you are doing to your own precious self when you don't give yourself the credit you deserve. Slow down, make a list of all of the things you have accomplished, and hug yourself. Not only will this help you to stay in the moment and relish the work you have put in, but it will help you realize that you *are* pretty kick ass, and your vibration/energy will rise up, bringing you more and more goodness.

USING YOUR GIFTS TO TEACH/LEAD

Before we dive into this next batch of info, I want you to know that one of the most important things to remember is that you can't teach others until someone is ready to accept the information. People can only accept the things that they are ready and prepared to accept, and it's *so* freaking important to meet people where they are. Even if you're excited to share your new happy life guide with everyone you come into contact with, your excitement could come off as overwhelming and pushy. Just like that little caterpillar that you once were, others are just starting their journey, and pushing them off the cliff to see if they can fly will only land them on the ground with some major trust issues.

So how do you know if someone is ready? Pay attention to the cues that they are giving off. Many times the people around you will notice the big change in you and ask what you're doing. When you pique curiosity, questions follow, and it's then that you can share some of your knowledge (and perhaps this book…*cough, cough*) with them. Don't be afraid to talk openly about the way you have transformed yourself, but watch for the cues that someone has become disengaged. One that sticks out for me is when someone you are speaking with starts saying, "Oh yeah?" while fumbling around or looking at their phone. I can usually tell when I've lost someone, and I save my breath. Two reasons: they are never going to hear what you're saying, and they aren't on your energy map. It's okay. It doesn't mean they are wrong and awful. It just means that they aren't where you are yet, growth-wise and energetically.

Teaching by example is a natural way to share your knowledge. If you are just walking around this earth doing you and seeing great results, people are going to notice and want to know what you're doing that is creating such a change. Think about it. There are thousands of fitness influencers out there. They look fit, healthy, happy, and successful. People naturally gravitate toward that kind of stuff. They want to know *how* that person got there so that they can feel fit, healthy, happy, and successful too. This is no different, and if you feel like you are in line with your best self and it's on your heart to share, then when this starts happening and people head your way, then you will know it's time.

Writing this book is actually my way of sharing with you. My gifts as a writer are being utilized to create a product for my personal development business in which I share with the world what I did to change my life and go from a lack mindset to a boss babe (Terry's words, not mine) with a growth mindset. When someone is ready to read it and dive in with me, they will. If they aren't ready, then this all might sound a little woo-woo. (gain, Terry's words, not mine. Ha!)

Through my public speaking career experience, I have learned that being really really real is going to touch the most people. It's hard to learn from someone who seems to have it all together. The successful career, the beautiful family…the perfect spray tan. (But is there really such a thing? I know even the most beautiful spray tans that I've received have come with a little streak here or there.)

Guiding people who are in the caterpillar phase with the lessons from the butterfly phase is going to be rough. They can't see themselves where you are, and they certainly can't see you where they are. This is why it's so important to tell your story and connect with those who are feeling the pull.

Here are a few things to keep in mind when you are ready to guide others.

1. CONTINUE TO BE AUTHENTIC AND GENUINE.

By this stage of your life, this should come naturally to you. A note about sharing your story and encouraging others: be sure that you are not giving everything away all at once. You worked hard for your wings and, although it is super important to be authentic and share what worked and what didn't, allowing people to make their own mistakes is crucial in their growth journey. There may also be a time when your ego wants to step in and create fear that if you guide someone, they may do better than you. Oh, little butterfly, remembering that there is room for everyone and that we are all on our own path will be extra important here, because if you can help someone along the way, not only will you be rewarded tenfold, but you will most likely learn more lessons that will continue *your* growth. Double whammy!

2. PROVIDE HONEST AND CONSTRUCTIVE FEEDBACK.

You aren't helping anyone if you are just yessing them to death. Remember to always give actionable solutions when pointing out a problem so that it doesn't come across as criticism.

When offering advice or feedback:

Be specific: provide detailed examples to illustrate your points, making it easier for the recipient to understand and act upon.

- Focus on behavior, not character: address actions and behaviors rather than making it personal, fostering a more positive and receptive environment.

Offer alternatives: suggest alternative approaches or solutions to problems, empowering individuals to make positive changes.

Use the "sandwich" method: surround constructive feedback with positive comments, creating a balanced and encouraging message.

- Encourage dialogue: foster open communication by inviting the other person's perspective and being willing to discuss the feedback.

- Remember, the goal is to support growth and improvement.

Another great way to support during the learning process is to encourage your mentee to explore lots of ideas, putting an emphasis on the importance of curiosity, open-mindedness, and the freedom to explore diverse thoughts. Encourage your caterpillar to embrace challenges, question assumptions, and be sure to share examples of how idea exploration has led to positive outcomes in your journey.

3. EMPATHY AND PATIENCE.

Empathy and patience are two essential qualities that contribute to meaningful human connections. Empathy involves the ability to understand and share the feelings of others, fostering a sense of compassion and connection. It allows individuals to see the world from different perspectives, promoting a deeper understanding of diverse experiences. On the other hand, patience is the virtue of remaining calm and tolerant, especially in challenging situations. It enables individuals to navigate conflicts with composure, fostering better communication and cooperation. Together, empathy and patience form a powerful combination that nurtures positive relationships and promotes a harmonious society. Basically, this will make you one kick-butt mentor!

It's going to get frustrating if someone asks you to help them create a life they love but then won't do the things that need to be done in order to do it. I can only imagine my personal trainer, palm to forehead right now, thinking of allll of the times that I do this, but yet she is both empathetic and patient while gently (but confidently) helping me overcome obstacles as she reminds me that, yes, squats are really necessary.

4. BUILDING TRUST.

Building trust takes time and effort. Here are some steps that can help in building trust:

Be reliable: be consistent in your actions and deliver on your promises. If you say you will do something, make sure you follow through.

Be honest and transparent: be truthful in your communication and don't hide information. Being open and transparent builds trust by showing that you have nothing to hide.

Be consistent in your behavior: act consistently in different situations, demonstrating integrity and reliability. Being predictable can help others feel more secure and confident in you.

Communicate effectively: clearly and honestly communicate your expectations, thoughts, and feelings. Miscommunication can lead to mistrust, so strive for clarity and understanding.

Practice active listening: show genuine interest in what others have to say and validate their feelings. Reflect back what you hear to ensure understanding and build trust.

Admit and learn from mistakes: owning up to mistakes and taking responsibility shows humility and a willingness to grow. Learning from mistakes and making changes builds trust in your ability to improve.

Demonstrate competence: show expertise and competence in your field. People are more likely to trust someone who demonstrates their knowledge and skills.

Respect confidentiality: respect others' privacy and keep sensitive information confidential. Being trustworthy in keeping secrets is an important aspect of building trust.

Be patient: trust takes time to build. It may not happen overnight, so be patient and consistent in your efforts.

Remember, building trust is an ongoing process that requires continuous attention and effort. It's important to be genuine, reliable, and open in your interactions to foster trust with others. Rock on!

In conclusion, helping others live their best lives is not just some bland responsibility—it's a freaking *profound* responsibility and a downright marvelous gift. We, the enlightened souls who have grown and conquered our own crap, get to be beacons of inspiration, shining a light on the foggy path for others to embark on their life-changing journeys.

But hey, it's not just about giving some half-hearted advice or half-assed guidance. No, no, no. It's about offering support, encouragement, and a wealth of knowledge. We create a cozy little haven where people can uncover their passions, talents, and unique strengths. We help them release those pesky societal expectations and all the useless limitations they've put on themselves. We empower them to embrace their true selves and live a life that really freakin' resonates.

Helping others live their best lives ain't no joke. It takes empathy, understanding, and the ability to connect deeply with their wildest dreams. We hold their hands through all the crap, celebrate their awesome achievements, and remind them that they are unstoppable.

By guiding others toward their best lives, we become total catalysts for change, sparking a fire that inspires everyone around them. When they step into their power and start kicking ass, they create a tsunami of positivity that forces others to sit up and take notice.

In the end, helping others live their best lives is a team effort. Our own personal growth is all intertwined with the growth of those we guide. Together, we redefine what success means, screwing the external measures and focusing on inner fulfillment. We say "screw you" to societal expectations and start living a life that aligns with our deepest values and passions.

So, let's keep on this kick-ass journey of guiding others to live their best lives. Let's inspire authenticity, courage, and self-discovery in every single damn person we meet. And by doing so, may we all find true fulfillment, joy, and meaning in our own lives, as well as in the lives we just happen to rock along the way. Boom!

Conclusion

As we bid farewell, my fabulous friends, I want to remind you that self-discovery is an endless and thrilling adventure. It's not just a destination, it's a lifelong roller coaster of unraveling who we are and embracing our freakin' fantastic gifts.

Throughout this book, we've delved deep into the core of self-discovery, ditching those lame limiting beliefs and societal expectations. We've explored the power of soul-searching, asking ourselves the tough-as-nails questions that uncover our passions and desires. We've connected to our authentic selves, celebrating the mind-blowing talents and abilities locked within.

Now, armed with this mind-blowing clarity, it's time to fearlessly leap toward living our most authentic lives. It's time to give ourselves the go-ahead to chase our passions, no matter how wild and unconventional they might seem. Remember, authenticity knows no bounds or restrictions.

On this crazy journey, it's vital to surround ourselves with a tribe of badass individuals who uplift and support us. We gotta find mentors and role models who've already embraced their true selves and are killing it authentically. Their guidance and wisdom will be like liquid gold as we navigate the obstacles and setbacks life throws our way.

Living authentically takes guts, resilience, and a commitment to personal growth. It means embracing vulnerability like a fearless warrior as we step out of our comfy zones and face our fears head-on. It means trusting our gut instincts, following our hearts, and staying true to our values, even when life throws a curveball.

Remember, setbacks aren't failures, they're chances for growth and self-discovery. They're freakin' invaluable lessons that help us refine our path and get back on track. So face these moments with grace and determination, knowing they'll lead you to personal development and ultimate bliss.

And as you walk this path toward authenticity, keep reevaluating and realigning yourself with your passions and purpose. Life keeps evolving, and so do we. What spoke to us before may not ignite the same fire within us now. Give yourself permission to embrace new interests, unearth hidden talents, and fine-tune your true calling.

In the end, living our best, most authentic lives is not just a gift to ourselves, it's also a massive inspiration to others. By embracing and nurturing our uniqueness, we're granting permission and empowering those around us to do the same. Your journey of self-discovery has the power to create a ripple effect, pushing others to uncover their gifts and unleash their authentic badassery.

As we bid adieu, remember that self-discovery is a lifelong commitment to embracing our true selves, not just a one-time destination. Embrace the journey, cherish every damn moment of growth, and never stop exploring the mind-blowing depths of your authenticity.

In the immortal words of the legendary Ralph Waldo

Emerson, "To be yourself in a world that is constantly trying to make you something else is the greatest accomplishment." So go out there and conquer, creating a life that screams your authentic self from the rooftops. Within you lies everything you need to live a life of purpose, fulfillment, and pure unadulterated joy. Seize this glorious opportunity, and let your light shine so freaking bright that the whole world can't help but be blinded by your awesomeness. Let's GLOW, baby!

xo Jmc

Thank You

Hey GLOW- GETTER,

This is for you

(Scan for your personalized custom Thank You video)

Acknowledgments

"I would like to extend my heartfelt gratitude to the following people who have played a crucial role in my journey. To my amazing husband, who has been my rock, supporting me and believing in my every crazy move, I am forever grateful. To my kids, who bring me joy and inspiration every day. To my Dad, who never fails to tell me how proud he is of me, I cherish your words. And to my friends, who let me ramble on and share my ideas with you, I appreciate your listening ears.

I also want to express my deepest appreciation to Christie Stratros, not only for being an exceptional editor, but also for being a true friend and confidant. Your guidance and expertise have been invaluable.

Lastly, I want to acknowledge the incredible Glendon Haddix, who has taught me more than I could have ever imagined possible. You may not realize it, but you are the conduit between people's dreams and reality. Your wisdom, experience, and kindness have had a profound impact on me, and I am forever changed because of our time working together.

Thank you all for your unwavering support, encouragement, and love. This book would not have been possible without you."

www.ingramcontent.com/pod-product-compliance
Lightning Source LLC
Chambersburg PA
CBHW030557080526
44585CB00012B/404